Camping
With Kids

Camping With Kids

Hundreds of Fun Things to Do

Simon McGrath
Editor-in-Chief at The Camping and Caravanning Club

To Paula, Tom and Elliot, who have shared so many
camping and outdoor adventures with me

Published by AA Publishing, a trading name of AA Media Limited,
Fanum House, Basing View, Basingstoke, Hampshire, RG21 4EA, UK.

www.theAA.com

A CIP catalogue record for this book is available from the British Library.

ISBN: 978-0-7495-7697-4

Editor: Donna Wood
Art Director: James Tims
Designer: Kat Rout
Illustrator: May van Millingen

Printed and bound in Singapore by 1010 Printing Group Ltd

A05447

Please note, references to 'tents' in this book generally apply to all forms
of camping including caravans, motorhomes, glamping and trailer tents.

 Activities with the umbrella symbol are particularly suitable for
wet weather.

Contents

Foreword

When you mention camping to people who have never done it before, I would bet my Big Agnes sleeping mat that most of them think about a sad-looking family crouched under a tarpaulin in a field in the pouring rain.

But we know better, don't we? In just the last 10 years camping has moved on hugely. It's no longer a survival sport, class boundaries have been smashed and the gear and equipment is barely recognisable from that of our grandparents' generation. "A carbon fibre-poled, ripstop polyester tent you say? Ooh, we didn't have those when I was a child."

Whether it's under canvas or in a caravan or motorhome, camping gives you that freedom to explore and you can be as basic or as bourgeois as you like. When I talk about the freedom to explore I'm not just talking about the ability to head anywhere you fancy in the country on a Friday night so you can unzip the tent and wake up to whatever amazing view you choose on Saturday morning. I'm also talking about delving into a bit of self-analysis and discovering more about you and your family. Multiple studies done all over the world have shown us that time spent outdoors and connecting to nature is enormously valuable on a psychological, emotional and physical level. The Camping and Caravanning Club did its own research back in 2015 with Plymouth University and a survey of 11,000 Club members, and it revealed that, according to their parents, children who camp at least once a year are happier, do better at school and are healthier.

To me, the most important mention in all of this is the children. According to DEFRA, the likelihood of a child visiting any green spaces at all has halved in a generation. That is a scary statistic. We don't all have to be tree huggers or hikers or climbers, or work for the National Trust as a Forest Ranger, but getting to know our natural environment is essential to our growth and understanding as human beings. Do your kids know that healthy soil is vital for healthy crops (our food)? That trees are the lungs of the world that soak up our dirty carbon and help regulate our climate? That the world needs fresh purified water to survive and it doesn't just come out of the tap or bottle? If they don't touch a tree, splash in a river and get their hands dirty hunting for insects and worms, they probably never will. Looking at an image on a tablet isn't the same as touching it and experiencing it.

Valuing nature is one of the most important things we can teach our children – and camping makes it easy. It can bring you closer to so many wonderful things, whether you're exploring somewhere new or simply want to better appreciate wildlife and nature – the birds, the deer, a forest, river, or a mountain. The greatest barrier for loads of parents is knowing where on earth to begin and how to keep the children entertained. This book breaks down those barriers by offering straightforward, easy ideas to help your children discover, or even rediscover, their fascination with the outdoor world.

For me, the trick with getting children involved in camping in the first place is to start small and work your way up. You might get yourselves a little pop-up tent to chuck in the garden. Encourage their friends and yours to get involved. As Simon suggests in this book, teach them how to build dens, or make tiny shelters with twigs for the snails and small critters. It'll show them how the real thing can be done when they're bigger.

Get them out collecting twigs, autumn leaves or anything else they can find and have fun turning them into artwork. Try them out balancing a stick in both hands walking along a low log – it's great for their stability and core strength and you can include friends to make it a team-building experience. I mentioned high-tech equipment earlier – you don't have to leave it all behind (although a digital detox comes highly recommended). You can use your tablet or smartphone to video what you see and find, as Simon suggests on page 156, or try some geocaching, which is basically a treasure hunt (show me an adult or child who doesn't love a treasure hunt). Once they're bitten by the bug (or even a real bug!) it'll open up a world of fun and possibility. It might be learning new skills such as how to build a fire, navigating on a country walk or identifying a constellation in the night sky. Improving co-ordination and problem-solving. Building confidence and creativity. Growing knowledge of geography and wildlife. There's so much.

I've worked with The Camping and Caravanning Club since 2009 and have been its President since 2013, and I've known Simon McGrath, the author of this book and the Club's Editor-in-Chief, for as many years.

From camping at Warwick Castle, where the noisy peacocks woke everyone up before the crack of dawn, to trudging around a rather wet but lively Keswick Mountain Festival in the Lake District, Simon and I have been promoting camping together to the masses for a fair old while now. In this book, he's collected a wide variety of inspirational ideas to help get our children caught up in the camping bug, the outdoors and the natural world around us.

The more of us who follow Simon's example and go that extra mile to get our children outside more often, the healthier, happier and more confident they will be. Camping with them can be the start of an exciting new family adventure.

Julia Bradbury
Television presenter, President of The Camping and Caravanning Club, and outdoor enthusiast

Introduction

Simon McGrath

....

**"What does come [when camping] is fresh air in abundance,
a surprising appetite... a wonderful power of sleeping,
an absence of colds, and a jolly mental freedom and content.
Time is always ahead of us in camp."**

Thomas Hiram Holding
Author of *The Campers' Handbook,* published in 1908, and founder of The Camping and
Caravanning Club

....

Thomas Hiram Holding was a pioneer in more ways than one. He helped create camping as a pastime – one that has stood the test of time and continues to grow in popularity more than a century on. A good number of his thoughts and reflections on the great outdoors are as relevant today as they were when he wrote them back in the 1900s.

In many ways, his views on experiencing and enjoying the natural environment are even more important now, as a growing focus on technology means that future generations of children risk becoming detached from the wonders of the natural world around them.

So step forward camping – your passport to a host of outdoor adventures and memorable experiences, big and small.

Camping encourages us to slow down, to stop and connect with the natural environment around us. It helps us to notice more, hear more, smell more and see more. It enables us to watch our children play as they make their own discoveries. And hear them laugh – what sound could be better?

Through the pages of *Camping With Kids* I want to inspire people to get outdoors and enjoy camping in all its forms – to do it responsibly and safely, and above all to have fun and create lasting memories. I want to see kids 'rewilding' – reconnecting with nature – and learning skills and knowledge that are at risk of getting lost in the mists of time.

Camping With Kids is for parents and guardians, and grandparents for that matter, who either want to get started with camping or head out more often into the countryside with their family. The book isn't a technical guide, its aim is to offer inspirational ideas, to encourage families with children to give it a go. I'm not a parenting psychologist, I'm just combining my experience as a dad who relishes the joys of camping and being outdoors with his family with a healthy dose of passion and creativity.

There are seven chapters, each with a central theme and packed with inspirational ideas for activities to take part in as a family, discovering what makes each other tick and enjoying the great outdoors.

Chapter 1, *Getting There & Pitching Up*, starts with a look at the fun that can be had just by pitching up in the garden. It then moves to the campsite. Erecting the tent or setting up the caravan is something that pulls the family together as all can chip in. So why not make it even more enjoyable with a few campsite pitching challenges? I also take a look at the more chic camping world of 'glamping' – imagine snuggling beneath reindeer pelts in a tipi and going 'off-grid' in an eco-friendly way – not to mention the increasingly popular festival camping. Anyone fancy a flower painted on his or her face?

The second chapter, *Reconnecting With Nature*, looks at how to literally run wild with the kids. Why not get up with the dawn chorus, tiptoe off the campsite and enjoy a breakfast picnic as the rising sun warms the countryside, or learn how to lay a cypher trail through a wood with clues that lead to a cache of 'treasure'? Ever tracked an animal? Well here's how. Learn how to navigate, climb a hill and then watch the clouds come and go (and understand if those clouds are about to give you a good soaking).

The third chapter, *Relearning Ancient Skills*, revisits skills mum and dad no doubt enjoyed learning as kids. Tie a bowline knot with edible laces of liquorice before eating it or carve your own tent peg. Never made a fire before? Well, now's the time to start. Then tell stories and sing a few songs to get the evening going.

Camping and games go hand in hand so Chapter 4, *Games & Activities*, suggests some great card and board games to play if the weather's bad. And if the sun is shining, get outside and create your own family quest in the countryside. There are plenty of natural materials around for art and crafts, so why not get creative by making a collage or even a rose-petal perfume? Alternatively, take a more modern approach and make a short video of campsite wildlife or set a family challenge to photograph the best bug and the funkiest wellies.

Chapter 5, *Night-Time Fun*, waits for the sun to set before coming up with a whole host of suggestions to get the family venturing out into the darkness for night-time walks, games and exploration. It's a time when the bats and badgers will be out looking for dinner. and the countryside becomes a very different, magical world. And who's up for a game of hide-and-seek by torchlight?

An active holiday in the countryside means healthy appetites all round. So Chapter 6, *Classic Campsite Cookery*, whets the appetite with a range of tasty recipes ideal

for the campsite. Want to create the best-ever bacon butty – the breakfast staple of the camper? Or make the ultimate hot chocolate, toast some scrummy s'mores or knock up an easy family feast over the campfire? Then look no further.

Lastly, Chapter 7, *Active Young Explorers*, gets everyone busy and reconnecting with wildlife. Ever gone fishing for lunch, cycle-camping, fossil-hunting or crabbing (a McGrath family fave)? Well, now's the time to get started. And to top it all, now that you've experienced so many fun new skills, why not challenge the family to go camping in each of the four seasons, with the goal of taking part in new activities along the way. What better way could there be to appreciate the countryside and the natural world around us?

Young people thrive when facing challenges. They need to push themselves to find out who they are and to experience a sense of achievement. They need to discover life and what living really means. As my sons Tom and Elliot tell me, life's an adventure – and who am I to disagree? So pack the tent into the car or load up the caravan and get out to explore and enjoy the beautiful countryside together. After all, happy children equal happy parents.

1
GETTING THERE
& PITCHING UP

> ## "Old hands recommend people to practise at home, in the back garden if there is no other place; to sleep out a few times, and cook a meal or two... If half-a-dozen self-inflicted lessons do not accomplish the desired end, they will, at any rate, give confidence."

Thomas Hiram Holding
Author of *The Campers' Handbook*, published in 1908,
and founder of The Camping and Caravanning Club

First-time family campers take note: you don't have to plunge straight in by heading to a campsite. Pitching a new tent – with its array of poles, guy lines, pegs and fabric – can be daunting for the inexperienced, particularly when surrounded by fellow campers watching you grapple with the guy ropes while sipping a cool beer outside their perfectly pitched tents. I've lost track of the number of stories I've heard from campsite managers who've watched parents wrestle unsuccessfully with their new purchase only to give up and pack the family back into the car and head for home, red-faced and minus their new tent.

Camping in the garden

One easy way to gain confidence fast when camping is literally on your own doorstep, albeit the back one. Camping in the garden is a fantastic way to introduce children to tents while Mum and Dad, not to mention the kids themselves, can practise pitching it in the first place. And there's the added bonus of having your own creature comforts such as a toilet and kitchen just a short walk away.

Garden camping can be the perfect gentle introduction to sleeping in a tent in a known environment where the only wildlife you're likely to hear, apart from the dawn chorus, is the occasional snuffling hedgehog or the neighbour's cat having an inquisitive scratch around the place. It can also give youngsters a small taste of independence and older children the chance to camp in the tent without Mum and Dad.

After a couple of nights spent under canvas, but only a few feet away from everything that's familiar, the whole family will be bursting with confidence and excitedly looking forward to their first camping adventure beyond the boundaries of the garden. You will be ready to set off to your chosen campsite. My sons Tom and Elliot have enjoyed nights camping in the garden on a number of occasions and even slept well – unlike their worrying Mum and Dad!

"Are we nearly there yet?"

So you've loaded up the car, it's packed to the rafters with camping kit, somehow the bikes are safely on the roof rack and, as an added bonus, there's even room for the children. Just.

That means you're halfway there – except you're not. You now face a daunting three-hour journey to the promised land that will no doubt take in all manner of road works, congestion, detours, and pit stops for toilet breaks, not to mention the lady on the 'sat nag' telling you where you should be going – assuming you can hear her above the din of the children arguing in the back.

Then, just when you're five minutes down the road, having had the obligatory 'who locked the front door?' conversation, it happens. A little voice from the back of the car innocently asks: "Are we nearly there yet?" There's still two hours 55 minutes to go and the realisation kicks in. That question will be repeated again and again until you arrive at the campsite. So how do you maximise the amount of time in between the question inevitably being repeated? What's the best way to stop your little loved ones in the back becoming 'hangry' (hungry and angry), help the miles roll by faster and ensure that you arrive at the campsite in a tranquil mood, on speaking terms with your partner, and with excited children in the back eager to help pitch up?

It feels like you've planned the camping trip for months, so don't fall at the last hurdle by forgetting to organise the travel time too – in both directions. There

are many cunning diversions in the following pages that, provided you've thought ahead and put in a little bit of prep, will transform the journey from hell into a fun-filled adventure that gets everyone in the holiday mood. After all, there are far more interesting games to play than 'I spy' which, let's face it, gets ever so slightly monotonous on a motorway.

Pitching up as a family

I'll admit it. I have been known to lose my sense of humour when pitching up at a campsite. For me it can be the most stressful part of a camping holiday. And for that I reluctantly blame my job.

I'm often fortunate enough to be testing a new tent, caravan or motorhome and I hate – really hate – instruction manuals, especially if poorly written. I'm an impatient sort and just want to skip the learning part and know exactly what I'm doing so that I can find a nice secluded pitch, put the kettle on, sit back, relax and get the holiday in full swing.

However, unless you're camping in pre-erected tents or static caravans you've got to pitch your own accommodation, whatever that may be, and set up camp. So instead of getting het up I've learned to embrace it. More importantly, I want the family to be pulling together, have some fun and above all, stop being a grouchy dad who's barking orders. In other words I discovered I needed to chill out a bit, be more 'in the moment', and enjoy the precious holiday time with my family – and that's perfectly achievable.

Sadly these days a whole host of daily distractions mean many families are spending less time together. But the good news is, camping is the perfect antidote. According to The Camping and Caravanning Club's Real Richness report in 2011, camping promotes family cohesion, satisfaction, fulfilment and a feeling of togetherness. The report's findings revealed that 81 per cent of campers said it brought them closer together as a family. Ninety-one per cent of kids who camp said spending time exploring the countryside with mum and dad made them happy, while 76 per cent of them noticed their parents had more time for hugs. I'm all for that. Three-quarters of camping youngsters also said their parents shouted less. Good news all round then.

If everyone in the family rolls up their sleeves and literally pitches in, then it brings us together in a way that's increasingly hard to find in everyday life. By becoming active campers, we all contribute and work towards the same goal – setting up camp. What a great way to start the holiday and it's probably more fun than you think, provided there aren't too many instruction manuals to hand.

Make pitching a game

Plenty of campsites have playgrounds, but try to avoid dropping the kids off there at the start. Instead, try to include them in pitching the tent. Encourage them to participate and not spectate.

Set pitching challenges against the clock, and add little prizes such as a treat from the sweet jar. Why not see who can inflate their airbed the quickest?

A favourite for my two sons is helping me whack in the tent pegs with a rubber mallet. It not only gets them involved with the pitching but also makes them more aware of the guy lines to avoid potential trips during the holiday. And what child doesn't like using a grown-up's hammer? These days we adults seem more reluctant to let our children learn how to use tools – which means we're effectively de-skilling the next generation. So if they're really young, let them take the pegs out of the bag and pass them to you. If they're a little older, let them untie the guy lines and help you hit in the pegs with the mallet. Learning how to build and make things is a vital part of anyone's personal development.

Glamp it up

Glamping – an amalgam of the words glamorous and camping – has rapidly grown in popularity. And there are many good reasons for it. Glamping enables people to dip their toes in the water before buying all their own camping kit. There are more home comforts (some might say a bit of bling) and perhaps even the prospect of a better night's sleep courtesy of a feather down pillow on a proper bed complete with warm duvet and reindeer pelt. It also means that regular campers can pitch up at a campsite while their less hardy friends and family stay in the glamping accommodation. There are many different kinds of unusual glamping accommodation that you can set up camp in, ranging from tree houses and Mongolian yurts to tipis and geodesic domes. I've even seen helicopters converted into glamping accommodation.

Glamping adds things that are sometimes beyond the essential, which means layers of comfort and decorative touches that aren't necessary but will enhance the experience for, or even encourage, a reluctant camper to sleep closer to nature at night. And that's the key thing – you'll still be able to step out of your shepherd's hut or unzip your safari tent and stare up at the night sky. Or be woken by the rising sun and dawn chorus.

However, don't lose sight of the camping aspect altogether. Instead, glamping is a good excuse to go 'off-grid'. Cooking and eating alfresco are all part of the experience. If you are staying on a glampsite, you may well have access to an outdoor pizza oven or be able to cook over an open fire using a tripod and a Dutch oven pot. What's in the pot can add to the glamour of the occasion. So ditch the baked beans because boeuf bourguignon or coq au vin are on the menu tonight – they're easy to cook and super-posh to nosh. Just don't forget the candelabra!

Festival fun

Camping, not to mention glamping, is often at the heart of the ever-popular festival. It provides easy accommodation at venues where everyone has a shared passion, be it the music on the stage, the fare in the food tents or the kids' entertainment.

Pitching up with like-minded folk can be a hugely hospitable activity and Camping and Caravanning Club members organise social camping rallies every weekend the length and breadth of the country.

Festivals aren't just about music. They offer a range of themes and there's a large selection of family-friendly options too. It pays to choose a festival wisely and that means one that's right for both you and your children. Parents may want to see their favourite band, while the kids just want to stay put in the playing area with their new friends. So remember to re-set your expectations about what you're able to do as a family. Start small. Buy a day pass to a low-key festival that offers plenty for the children to enjoy and camp nearby to escape the crowds. And then build up from there. It's a wonderful introduction to camping for the whole family.

Camping in the garden

1
Check the weather

When camping in the garden, pick a night when the weather is forecast to be mild and dry to ensure the whole family has the best chance of enjoying their first night under canvas.

2
Watch an expert

Before you even tip it out of the bag, learn how to pitch the tent via the internet – many manufacturers post helpful videos online, which can make deciphering the written instructions so much easier.

3
Work together

Get the children involved with both pitching the tent and laying out their bedding. Make an effort to work together as a family to ensure your new home has everything you need.

4
Pitch up early

Erect the tent nice and early in the day so the children can have fun playing in it before settling down – tents make exciting dens.

5
Make it fun

Glamp up your tent during the day with bunting, fluffy rugs and outdoor fairylights (see page 34 for more ideas). Cook dinner on the barbecue in the garden, then make a champion hot chocolate before bed (see our recipe on page 212).

6
Have a torch to hand

Head torches are ideal for children in case they wake in the middle of the night. And it's always worth a quick reminder to switch off the torch before settling down and to put it in a memorable place.

7

Outdoor sleepovers

Plan an exciting, fun-filled birthday party sleepover under canvas. Just set a 'lights out' time – and remember to tell the neighbours first!

8

Sleeping like a dog

Pets can be uncertain of new experiences, just like children. So why not introduce your pooch to camping this way too – I did. Our golden retriever Monty had a bout of the 'zoomies' when he first came face-to-face with a tent in the garden, but is now happy sleeping in all manner of camping accommodation (although his snoring has been known to keep us awake).

Things to remember...

POP TO THE LOO
Remind everyone to make a last visit to the loo before snuggling down for the night.

TEDDY COMES TOO
For the younger ones, don't forget to bring their favourite cuddly toy or blanket camping too.

BE PREPARED
Make sure the route back to the house is clear of obstructions so that, if necessary, you can carry them back to their own beds without tripping over something in the dark.

KEY MOMENT
If they're garden camping without you, consider giving them a key to let themselves in for a loo visit or to clamber back into their usual bed.

"Camp is an introduction to a world in which happiness does not depend on circumstances or on money, but on developing one's own capacity for simple, healthy enjoyment. By treating the minor hardships and difficulties of camp life as a joke, seeds of grit, a sense of proportion and of humour are implanted."

Campcraft for Girl Guides, 1953

Are we nearly there yet?

9
Off we go!

When the time comes to try camping for real, think in advance of the types of games and books your children will enjoy en route – and remember to pack them.

10
Plan a detour

Factor in an interesting short trip to an attraction along the route to the campsite. Who doesn't love a picnic lunch in a pretty park or near some castle ruins? It's a guaranteed mood-lifter for young and old alike.

11

In-car entertainment

Audio books are great for young minds to visualise stories. Roald Dahl and David Walliams stories are particularly good when read out loud, and books with pop-up pictures add an extra dimension to reading. Reusable children's stickers can be great on rear windows to create imaginative games and stories.

12
Arms and legs

Split into teams and take it in turns to look out for pub signs, then count up the total number of arms and legs you've spotted and use that to accumulate a score. The Red Lion has four legs, and therefore equals four points, while the Dog and Duck notches up six points. Pub names such as The Royal Oak and The Windmill score nothing at all, nor do all those Slugs and Lettuces!

13
Stop off on the way

Call in on friends or family for a strategic cuppa. It's always good to see old friends – especially if they have kids of a similar age who can take yours off to play for a while. Our home is regularly used as a service station by camper friends whenever they're travelling the length of the country, since we live less than 10 miles from the M1.

14
Have hourly games

Plan a new game for each hour of the journey and try to hold out for as long as possible until you announce the next activity.

15

It's a wrap

Wrap up sweets or little games in several layers of paper, like a miniature 'pass the parcel'. We did this once on a long-haul flight and found it could take up to 10 minutes for little hands to remove the wrapping paper. It adds an element of surprise and those 10 minutes all add up.

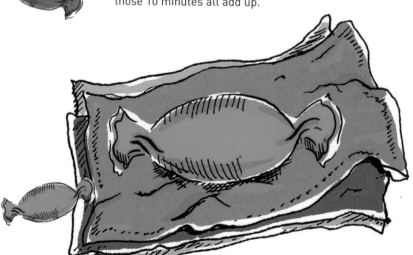

16
Know the score

Always have a notepad and pen in the glove compartment so you can keep score when playing games in the car.

17
Keep something back

Ensure there's a favourite toy easily to hand but out of sight. When things get grouchy it's a case of 'Look what I found!'

18

The number plate game

Memorise the last letters of a passing car's number plate and turn those letters into a three-word phrase. NTM could be: "Nearly There Mum?" while NAC is "Not A Chance!"

19
Agree the rules

Competitive games in the car can be great fun but they can also end in tears. Make sure you agree the rules at the start to avoid arguments.

20

Shopping list

It's a classic memory game. The person who starts says, "I went to the shops today and bought... four apples." The next person joins in and adds, "I went to the shop today and bought... four apples and a bag of tent pegs." See how long you can keep it going. It's good for the brain.

21
Pack the snacks

Take plenty of healthy drinks and snacks – eating and drinking keeps them busy too.

22
Family singsong

Don't rely on the car's stereo for musical entertainment. Exercise your vocal chords with a family singsong (see also page 115). All together now: "We're all going on a..."

23
Alphabet animals

Starting with A, take it in turns to name an animal starting with that letter. You could score the game, awarding bonus points for difficult letters and also helping someone if they're stuck.

24
The game of last resort

This is also known as the silence game. When all else fails, who can keep silent for the longest? Literally a great peacemaker.

25
Car bingo

Everyone in the car picks a colour that's a little different to the common ones (so silver is banned). Set a target and see who spots the number of vehicles of their chosen colour first. When they spot a car they have to call out their colour, and when they reach the target they must shout "bingo!". Alternatively, see who gets the most in a specified time limit.

bingo! bingo! bingo! bingo! bingo! bingo! bingo! bingo!

Pitching up

Handy hints...
Setting up camp

MAKE A ROTA

Remember the duty rota at Scout or Guide camp? Well, you could introduce one that doesn't sound as strict but ensures each member of the family is responsible for certain chores – children are good at recycling stuff, for example – and then swap them around regularly to keep it interesting. Create a points chart with stars on it and give them a small reward at the end of the holiday.

PILE ON THE PRAISE

Offer plenty of encouragement and praise for a job well done. Remember, it doesn't really matter if they get more water on themselves than in the drinking water container.

26
Bring a windbreak

Windbreaks are useful bits of kit that can segregate cooking areas from little ones, or create a bit of privacy where it's needed. They can also be used to create a play area or den.

27
Use a tarp

Tarpaulins, known as tarps, are fantastic bits of multi-purpose camping kit. Get the children to help set up a tarp as a shelter from any inclement weather. The area underneath becomes a very cosy den.

28
Share the responsibility

Camping involves a variety of different equipment, so why not encourage everyone to be responsible for looking after their own kit. Not just setting it up but maintaining and cleaning it. That could be as simple as a sleeping bag – understanding the best way to pack it back into a stuff sack and then airing it when home.

29

Take your compass

Why? Because if you pitch the tent with the front door facing east, the rising sun will warm the living area and work its way through the tent. It's far nicer to poke your head out of the tent early in the morning and feel the warmth of the morning sun on your face than unzipping the door to a chilly side that's cast in shadow.

30
Find the tap!

Most large campsites supply a handy map of the site. Ask if you can have one for each young camper and set a challenge to be first to find the drinking water tap. Or get into teams and allocate a list of places to find. If someone in each group has a smartphone, take a selfie as proof that you found them. Better still, give each team a camera to use. Or for more creative campers, challenge them to draw their own site map (remember to pin it to your fridge back home as a reminder of your camping adventure).

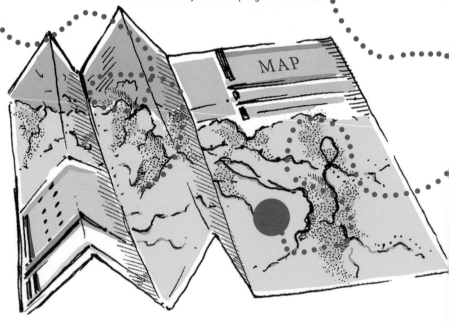

31
Study new designs

Take a look at the many different products on the market aimed at camping kids. Lots of kit has been designed with young children in mind over the last few years, from kid-sized camping chairs to animal-themed bedrooms in tents.

32
Build a bedroom

Get your youngsters to take full responsibility for setting up their bedroom and bed (and remembering where their cuddly toys and torches are too).

33
Packing away

It's the worst part of a camping holiday but ensure you get all the family involved with that too, not to mention the cleaning and drying back home. Best not get the younger ones to empty the toilet cassette you find in caravans and motorhomes. Unfortunately, some jobs are best left to the grown-ups.

Things to remember...

TIME AND PLACE
If the kids are going off exploring without you, be sure you all agree on a realistic time and a familiar place to meet.

FLY THE FLAG!
Back at the tent, make sure you've made your temporary new home easily recognisable (see page 39). It's amazing how similar a row of tents can look in unfamiliar surroundings, so think about decorating it in some way or flying a home-made flag.

TRIP HAZARDS
Point out any electricity hook-up cables that could be a trip hazard.

Glamping

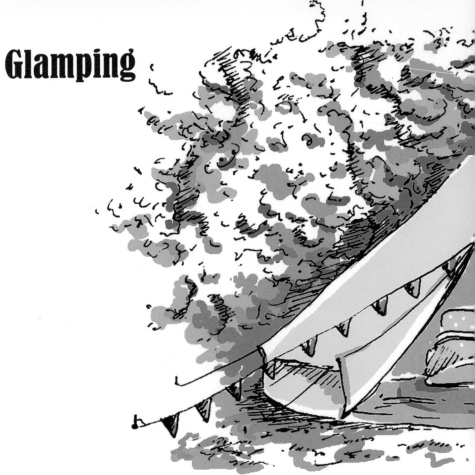

34

Glamp up your tent

Dream up ways to glamp up your own tent with the help of your little ones. Think plush, think unnecessary. Think bean bags, rugs, warm blankets and scatter cushions. Forget minimal packing – glamping is about going overboard with added style.

Solar-powered fairy lights are widely available and don't need batteries. Buy a plain tipi and decorate it with your own funky artwork (using waterproof paint, of course). Paint empty jam jars and use them for tea lights, keeping them outside for warm evenings. Smarten up the table with a colourful cloth and napkins.

Take along a small chalkboard and write an inspiring thought for the day, a list of birds and flowers to spot or a

35

Make some bunting

family activity challenge. Avoid writing the list of chores – you're glamping after all. And you don't have to head to a campsite. Why not step outside the backdoor and go garden glamping?

There are plenty of options to buy bunting online, but it's much more fun for the kids to make their own and there's no need for glue. Simply tie lots of colourful fabric strips in neat knots to a long, sturdy piece of string and drape it over your tent or caravan.

> "I have just visited an ideal family camp. It is on an island in a river. There was the eating tent, the sleeping tent, the servant's tent, the cooking tent for wet weather, and the over-boat tent. Here the family and their servants were spending a 'savage' holiday... They were having a delightful time."

Thomas Hiram Holding
Author of *The Campers' Handbook*, published in 1908, and founder of The Camping and Caravanning Club

36

Take a vase

Mum gets a lie-in while dad secretly whisks the kids off early in the morning on a flower hunt. Pick a handful of common flowers from meadows or hedgerows and arrange them in a vase (avoid protected species and don't pick from land such as nature reserves). Put the vase on a suitably glamorous tray together with mum's breakfast. How about smoked salmon and scrambled eggs with freshly snipped chives? That will certainly win dad some Brownie points.

37

Get some glamping accessories

There's a vast array of glamping kit to add that extra touch of luxury to your tent, from funky inflatable seats to mini portable speakers and portable filter coffee-makers.

38

Glamp up your picnic

Don't let the side down when you go for a stroll and a picnic lunch. Think wicker hampers, bright picnic rugs, lightweight foldable chairs and even ornate stakes for the ground that will hold either your bottle of wine or glass. Canapé anyone?

Handy hints...
Live the high life

The Camping and Caravanning Club has its own network of Ready Camp safari-style tents that are ideal for a spot of glamping. Here's a selection of other accommodation to also look out for when glamping...

- Camping pods
- Cabins and barns
- Helicopters (camp in a 'copter)
- Pre-pitched restored VW campervans, classic caravans, and Airstreams
- Shepherd's huts
- Geodesic domes (my sons called this 'doming')
- Gypsy caravans
- Tree houses
- Yurts (also known as 'gers')
- Tipis
- Bell tents

Festival Fun

39

Stage your own mini festival

Creating your own festival for friends and family is a good introduction and much of the fun is in the planning. Pitch up in a friend's large garden that can take a few tents and invite along two or three families.

Ask each family to organise a craft activity, nature trail or storytelling session for the daytime. When the evening draws in, each family also has to stage some form of entertainment such as music, a show or stand-up comedy act.

Don't forget to give your festival a glamorous name and make some tickets, wristbands and draw up a programme of events. Then decorate the tents with bunting, flags and outdoor fairy lights.

40

Use potato pegs

Festival campers often accidentally leave metal tent pegs in the ground, which is a hazard for farm animals such as cows. Instead, use biodegradable starch tent pegs made from potato.

41

Paint a face

Buy some face paints and have a go yourself. Flowers and butterflies are colourful and easy, and fit well with the festival spirit.

Things to remember...

DON'T OVERDO IT

Festivals can be both daunting and exhausting for children, especially little ones. A friend's pedometer showed she once clocked up 17 miles in a day at a festival, which is a whopping distance for little legs. So plan accordingly and try not to get carried away.

HAVE A MISSING PERSON PLAN

Festivals are busy places, so ensure everyone knows what to do if people get split up. On arrival decide on a meeting point. Ensure everyone has each other's mobile phone number. Get children a wristband that contains contact information or write Mum and Dad's numbers on their arm. And double check the festival site has a mobile signal.

PROTECT LITTLE EARS

Kids' ears tend to be more sensitive than adults, so take along some ear defenders for them when visiting noisy music festivals.

42

Make a flag

Festivals and flags go well together. Flags are easy to make and fun to fly and having one by your tent makes it easy to get back to base when confronted with a sea of tents.

Flags are about identity, so think about how you want to represent your family and ensure it stands out from the rest. Why not design a unique family coat of arms?

The easiest way to make a flag is to cut a piece of plain fabric into a rectangular shape. It will be subjected to the weather, so ensure the materials including paints are suitable for outdoor use. If there's little or no wind, how will the flag look? This is where the canton section, the top inner square of a flag, can be used to ensure it is identifiable even when hanging limp. Look up the flags of America, Australia or New Zealand to see examples of cantons.

Use colours that work well together and keep the design reasonably simple without too much detail. The flag could be divided into quarters, each with a design created by a different family member. Remember to repeat the design on the flip side of the flag.

The flag could simply be tied to the tent itself. However, a flag pole will give greater visibility, though you'll need to consider what the pole will be made of (telescopic poles pack away neatly), how it will be safely secured,

perhaps using a ground stake, and how the flag will be attached to withstand the wind – this could be done by making fabric loops, using Velcro tabs, or glueing the flag to the pole. Alternatively, create a sleeve on the inside edge of the flag by folding over the fabric and stitching up the edge of the fold and along the top, into which the pole is inserted.

Test your creation at home in the wind and get set to show off the design at the festival.

Handy hints...
Family festival kit

DON'T FORGET TO PACK:

- Wet wipes and loo roll
- Hats, sun cream and sun glasses
- Refillable water bottles
- A pair of walkie-talkies. Fun to use and you can stay in touch with the kids
- Glow sticks or torches
- Good boots or wellies with thick socks
- Plenty of layers
- A rain poncho, which can also be sat on or draped over several people
- Trolley to transport kit from the car to the camping field
- First-aid kit

43

Stand out from the crowd

Tents, especially A-frame styles, are increasingly being made with funky and colourful designs. The traditional blues, greens and khakis are still popular, but a number of more creative designs have been putting in appearances on campsites and at festivals and other outdoor events in recent years and in ever-increasing numbers. A colourful tent that expresses your personality is fun and – importantly – helps you and the kids find your tent in a crowded campsite or festival field. So come on – find your creative streak and get decorating.

2
RECONNECTING WITH NATURE

> # "The camp gives this – exercise without fatigue, fresh air night and day, and sufficient excitement to create interest, and remind a man that he lives."
>
> Thomas Hiram Holding
> Author of *The Campers' Handbook*, published in 1908,
> and founder of The Camping and Caravanning Club

I always used to smile to myself when I arrived at my old sailing club to be greeted by a sign warning motorists to 'Beware free-range children'. The sad reality is that our children's roaming radius is shrinking at an alarming rate, according to the Wild Network, a venture that aims to 're-wild' childhood by reconnecting youngsters with nature.

It's a complex subject but the area in which our children venture out, play and explore has reduced dramatically in recent generations. A film called *Project Wild Thing* assesses the impact that staying indoors and looking at screens of one sort or another has upon our children. One of the central questions it poses is what would happen if a generation became completely disconnected from nature.

Step forward camping. The great thing about spending a night under canvas is that it quite literally brings us closer to nature and the countryside by introducing us to the feeling of lumpy ground beneath our roll mat or dew-covered grass between our toes, the sound of birdsong early in the morning or the snuffle and grunts of an inquisitive hedgehog at night; the fresh smell of grass or forest trees making our nostrils tingle. Campsites also provide a natural extension to children's roaming radius. Camping breaks us away from the routines and distractions of home and reminds us of the simple pleasures in life, such as rolling down a hill or gazing at the night sky.

On one of my camping trips, both adults and teenagers decided to get to our destination a little faster by rolling down a hill. The fresh smell and prickly feel of meadow grass up close is a simple yet powerful way to start that rewilding process. It was spontaneous, fun and left a lasting impression on us all. I'm not sure it got us to the bottom any quicker, but if ever there was a snapshot that summed up running wild, it was this.

Early rising
Sunrise is a magical part of the day. Generally, we're more likely to see the sun set, and yes, they are fabulous to witness. But nothing compares to glimpsing the first

colourful rays of sunshine as they slowly spill over the horizon. It heralds the start of a new day and that day is there ahead of you, waiting to be filled with adventure and enjoyment.

The campsite brings us closer to nature, starting with the inevitable dawn chorus. Although you're stirring thanks to the crescendo of birdsong and sunlight, it's tempting to snuggle back down into your sleeping bag, pulling the hood back over your head to block out any light. But don't. Resist the urge to sleep just a little more. Instead embrace the best part of the day. Get the kids up and witness the countryside and wildlife as it comes to life. It's a wonderful time to see and hear birds as they sing before their breakfast.

Leave off your shoes and feel the cold early morning dew on the grass on your bare feet before the sun dries it up. Or listen to the early morning frost crunch underfoot. This is such a simple way to connect with nature, to reacquaint ourselves with our surroundings. Night owls – and maybe even teenagers – will be converted by the best time of the day. And the chances are that no-one else will be there to experience it with you except your family.

Picnic for breakfast

Who said picnics were for lunch or tea? Climb a hill in that early morning mist and light, and take along a family picnic for breakfast. Then watch the sun rise over your cornflakes while you enjoy the dawn chorus.

Make sure you prepare the picnic the night before and have it all ready in a bag. Lay out everyone's clothes too and put on lots of layers as it is a chilly time of day. You

can always remove layers as you – and the day – warm up. Remember your flasks and it's always worth setting everything up for tea- and coffee-making the night before so that all you have to do is strike a match to light the stove.

As you set off on your mini adventure, remember to go quietly to avoid waking up the rest of the campsite – kids love to do exaggerated tip-toeing. That way you'll have the countryside all to yourself.

Join in with the dawn chorus

The first birds start warming up about an hour before the sun rises (about 4am in spring) and for a while the singing gets progressively louder as the day gets older. Skylarks, blackbirds, robins and song thrushes are early starters with smaller birds such as wrens joining in later. All that singing takes some energy and so it's the fittest, hardest working male birds that are the most impressive. They have to be – they're looking to impress a mate. The singing tails off as the day warms up and the birds use the brighter light to go in search of food.

When a tent becomes a bird hide

I once camped on the shore of a reservoir with my then young son Tom in a small dome tent. We awoke really early and carefully unzipped our tent to get that 'first view' moment often talked about by campers – the scene that lies before them which will create lasting memories. This one didn't disappoint – Tom and I soon realised that our tent had become a bird hide overnight. The reservoir was as still

as a millpond as swans and geese swam effortlessly by just a few yards away, completely unaware or unconcerned about our presence.

Experience a cloud inversion

They're tantalisingly rare and require a very early start. The rewards for the lucky few, however, are dazzlingly beautiful views of a seldom-seen spectacle of nature – the cloud inversion.

A cloud inversion is formed when cold fog is trapped in the bottom of a valley by a layer of warmer air. If you head for the heights you'll eventually emerge in warm sunshine looking back down on a sea of cloud hugging the valley walls.

To increase your chances of experiencing a cloud inversion you'll need to camp in places such as the Lake District, Snowdonia and mountainous areas of Scotland. Pitching up in autumn or winter will improve your prospects further still.

Check the weather forecast the night before. To be in with a chance of seeing a cloud inversion you'll need a combination of light winds, cold temperatures and high pressure. A light haze that hangs in the sky at dusk may also be a sign.

If the conditions are right, your best bet is to pick a hill that's ideally at least 500 metres high and start walking upwards before dawn breaks. You should emerge from the cloud somewhere between the 300 to 600 metres mark with the sun

rising as a new day dawns. All that's left to do is find a comfy spot, unpack your breakfast picnic and drink in the incredible views.

Book a pitch at a campsite near Derwentwater in the Lake District, for example, keep your fingers crossed for the right weather conditions, and hike up the nearby fells called Cat Bells – Beatrix Potter country – which at 451 metres high should hopefully give you and the children a grandstand view.

Boot camp

It's amazing how far little legs can travel, especially when there are rewards around each corner. A countryside walk doesn't have to be a dull plod from one place to another. Far from it. With a little creativity and planning, walking can provide endless days out or short excursions with the added bonus of exercise, fresh air, big views and the chance to get closer to nature.

Country walks take you away from the noise and danger of roads and bring you much closer to nature, where senses become more heightened. You become attuned to your surroundings, whether picking up the smell of wild flowers, hearing the noise of a distant animal, or catching a glimpse of movement in a tree out of the corner or your eye. That's why it's the number-one pastime for members of The Camping and Caravanning Club. And they should know.

Getting lost... and found again

The countryside is a wonderful place to explore, and finding your way from one place to another is fun, sometimes challenging, occasionally tiring but ultimately always rewarding.

I once spent a day trekking on my own through the Samaria Gorge on the island of Crete. It's about eight miles long and 300 metres deep in places and although navigation was straightforward – keep following the gorge until you hit the village of Agia Roumeli and the Mediterranean Sea – at one point it posed an unusual challenge. The dried riverbed was boulder-strewn and although there was a path it was almost impossible to follow through the rocks. Just when I thought I'd found it, I lost it again and had to struggle over large rocks that were tough on my feet and ankles. The answer was staring at me every 20 metres or so – big piles of donkey dung. Mules trek up and down the gorge regularly and they were going to know where the path ran. So I found myself walking from one pile of dung to another, much like using cairns on hills and mountains, as they accurately marked the trail until I was clear of the boulder field.

Being able to navigate and developing 'hill skills' are not only important but great fun to learn too. They equip us with the knowledge to safely and responsibly enjoy the great outdoors – and are skills we can easily pass on to future generations. But remember to watch out for the piles of dung, in more ways than one!

Climb a hill

Go a step further and a few steps higher. Hills and mountains have something magical, perhaps even spiritual, about them. They dominate the skyline, look inviting in summer and moody in winter (and sometimes the other way around too). They take effort and commitment to climb and in exchange offer rewards in the shape of a sense of achievement and fantastic views – clouds permitting – for the few who venture up them. And it often is a few. I've climbed hills and mountains with my family and felt that we had both the summits and the views to ourselves.

As remote and extreme places they should not be feared but certainly respected. All who venture into them have a responsibility to learn hill skills, have the right preparation, fitness levels and equipment to be self-reliant. Learning the skills and gaining the experience is all part of the fun, challenge and ultimately the reward.

The wonder of the weather

When we think of the countryside we imagine hills, fields, trees and wildlife. But let's not forget the landscape around us has been shaped by the weather.

The ever-changing cloud has fascinated daydreamers and meteorologists in equal measure. Clouds create skyscapes that are stunning to look at and hold clues to what the weather has in store.

49

The weather means much more than the feeling of wind in our hair and the rain on our face. It can influence our daily movements and affect our moods. And dare I say it, the weather can also put a damper, quite literally, on a camping holiday.

That said, the weather is there to be marvelled at and understood – it's a way to tune in with our environment when enjoying the great outdoors. Forecasting the weather is a useful skill to learn – you may rely on it to plan your outing, decide on which clothes to wear, or make important decisions to stay safe, warm and dry while in the countryside, especially on hills and mountains where the weather can take a turn for the worse very quickly.

It's fun to learn more about the rain (who said puddles were to be avoided?), the temperature, wind, pressure and visibility. Children can also learn that Mother Nature is on hand to give them a few fun pointers. Why not learn a few meteorological skills and become a sky-watcher?

Mindfulness

The weather is not the only thing that can affect our moods. Increasingly we hear of mental health issues affecting children and young people. That life gets busier and more stressful. And that we are seeing a generation becoming more disconnected with their natural environment. However, there is help at hand and it's called mindfulness. What is it? I've read various definitions of mindfulness but they come back to the same things: being aware of your immediate surroundings and thoughts, and being – living – in the moment. Mindfulness is deliberately focussing upon the 'here and now' rather than worrying about the future or the past. On a campsite that means being aware that you've been woken by the dawn chorus and listening to it, for example. Or enjoying the feeling of wet grass from early morning dew on your bare feet and smelling the bacon as it sizzles in readiness for someone's breakfast.

Health experts tell us mindfulness improves overall wellbeing, and helps tackle anxiety and depression. It helps children and teens cope with their emotions, it improves sleep, better equips them to deal with stress, improves concentration, and assists physical relaxation. Adults too need to escape from the hustle and bustle of everyday life and that means mentally as well as physically, so why not learn mindfulness together? Camping and being outdoors in the fresh air, with the sights and sounds of nature all around, makes for an ideal setting to improve mindfulness and wellbeing. But don't just take it from me.

Ever heard of 'tent therapy'? In the early 1900s, tuberculosis patients in the US had to be quarantined from other patients by camping in hospital grounds. When their mental attitudes and physical conditions improved far faster than expected, doctors put it down to living in tents. Clearly they were on to something – a greater immersion in nature and a simpler, pared-down way of living.

More recently The Camping and Caravanning Club's Real Richness report found that 89 per cent of campers surveyed said that they had found that camping relieved stress. Eighty-four per cent of adult campers felt the pastime was good for a child's health. In a nutshell, the report concluded that camping really made people happier.

Naturally yoga

Camping is an opportunity to wake with the birds and rise with the sun. So why not use that period of peace and tranquillity to combine it with yoga – one of the oldest-known natural therapies for mind, body and spirit.

Yoga is good for physical and mental health. It slows us down and makes us mindful. It is also becoming increasingly popular with children who can take it forward into adult life. Experts say the many benefits of yoga for kids includes calming the mind, developing co-ordination and balance, and boosting concentration. It can help equip youngsters with the skills to tackle issues that we all inevitably face and to cope with higher stress levels from exams.

Yoga is also very in tune with the natural world and because camping brings us closer to nature, the two go well together. Why not learn it as a family?

Run wild

44
Roll down a hill

Pick a suitable hill, have a quick look around for obstacles (and animal poo), fold your arms across your chest, and go for it. Great for races. And temporary dizziness.

46
Make a mud pie

Scoop a chunk of mud into a bucket and remove any stones, twigs and leaves, not to mention worms. Add water, mix with a stick to get a nice gloopy clay-like consistency. Mould into fun shapes and decorate with those discarded stones, twigs and leaves. Go on! Get your hands dirty.

45
Climb a tree

Ensure the branches of the tree are strong enough and shoes have good grip. Start small, don't venture too high, stay close to the trunk and climb back down again, the best way usually being the route you went up by. Climbing trees teaches planning, risk assessment, and builds confidence. Elms and oaks are good species to climb. And if you really get into it, try a tree-based aerial obstacle course complete with rope ladders, cargo nets and zip wires.

47

Go orienteering

The aim of orienteering is to navigate between control points using a specially drawn map in a defined sequence to get the best time. Participants can walk or run, but they must decide the best route to complete the course.

The beauty of orienteering is that it can be done anywhere from a remote forest to a playground – or a campsite – and all the family can join in. Orienteering builds confidence and family members can work together to make decisions (how do we navigate around that prickly hedge?). Kids get a buzz when they locate a control point, where cards are marked or clipped as proof it's been found, before plotting their route to the next one. Visit www.britishorienteering.org.uk for further information.

48

Get out geocaching

This is a modern-day treasure hunt using GPS devices (those downloaded to smartphones will do fine) and there are several million active geocaches around the world to find.

To participate, you will need to sign up for a cost-free subscription to a geocaching website such as www. geocaching.com, and load the chosen co-ordinates into a GPS device. Part of the challenge is to find the best route to the location – there may be a river or other obstacles in the way.

The geocache is usually a small plastic box often containing small trinkets. Once found, you can take a trinket but you should leave an item of the same or greater value. You then fill out the logbook and also log it online.

Things to remember...

KEEP IT POSITIVE

We want our children to run wild but they still need boundaries. So set those boundaries but in a way that's positive rather than negative. Instead of telling them what they can't do, talk about the things they can do.

SET THE LIMITS

Campsites are considered safe places for kids to go off exploring, playing and making new friends, but always agree a safe, known meeting place and a time to be there before they go off exploring.

FLY THE FLAG

Big sites will have lots of tents, caravans and motorhomes that can all look the same to a small pair of eyes, and even grown-up ones, so ensure they know how to spot yours. Dress it up with identifiable marks or even fly your own flag. And dress kids in brightly coloured clothing so you can spot them easier.

"Nothing is more beautiful than the loveliness of the woods before sunrise."

George Washington Carver
Scientist and Inventor, 1864–1943

49

Swap roles

You're never too old to be young so swap roles with your children for the day! Breakfast is a good time to discuss the plans and let your youngsters make the decisions. Talk about what they would like to have achieved by the end of the day. What memories do they want to take away with them from being in charge? Let that family chat guide them as they decide what fun to have in the day ahead.

50

Kids run the kitchen

For one day, let the kids decide what meals you'll eat and what time you will eat them. This change in role means they should take over the cooking duties and the washing up too. In return they'll get a sense of responsibility – and perhaps even the option of having two ice creams in one day. Kids don't usually keep an eye on time so let time stand still. Ditch the watches, eat when you're hungry, sleep when you're tired.

51

Walkie-talkies

If you're encouraging your children to go off playing and exploring, you may want to stay in touch. Mobile phones are great for this and let's face it, most children have them from a certain age. However, they're not half as much fun as walkie-talkies for both parents and kids. Think about buying a child-friendly set to give children a greater sense of independence.

52

Be a 'spotter'

Walkie-talkies also add fun to hiding games as they can be used to give clues pointing towards the concealed location. Alternatively, one child with a handset could be a 'spotter' in the distance communicating instructions for the best way to evade capture to his or her friend who also has a handset.

53

Morse code

Use a walkie-talkie set to learn Morse code, a fantastic invention from the past. Kids can have great fun deciphering what their friends or parents are trying to tell them in code – in a dash!

	Code
A	● ▬
B	▬ ● ● ●
C	▬ ● ▬ ●
D	▬ ● ●
E	●
F	● ● ▬ ●
G	▬ ▬ ●
H	● ● ● ●
I	● ●
J	● ▬ ▬ ▬
K	▬ ● ▬
L	● ▬ ● ●
M	▬ ▬
N	▬ ●
O	▬ ▬ ▬
P	● ▬ ▬ ●
Q	▬ ▬ ● ▬
R	● ▬ ●
S	● ● ●
T	▬
U	● ● ▬
V	● ● ● ▬
W	● ▬ ▬
X	▬ ● ● ▬
Y	▬ ● ▬ ▬
Z	▬ ▬ ● ●
1	● ▬ ▬ ▬ ▬
2	● ● ▬ ▬ ▬
3	● ● ● ▬ ▬
4	● ● ● ● ▬
5	● ● ● ● ●
6	▬ ● ● ● ●
7	▬ ▬ ● ● ●
8	▬ ▬ ▬ ● ●
9	▬ ▬ ▬ ▬ ●
10	● ▬ ▬ ▬ ▬ ▬ ▬ ▬ ▬ ▬ ▬

54

Yoghurt pots

Don't despair if you haven't got a
walkie-talkie set. You can improvise
with younger children by making
your own using two empty yoghurt
pots with a small hole in each bottom
through which string is threaded and
tied between the two. Remember to
keep the line taut and while one child
speaks into their cup, the other puts
theirs to their ear to listen. See how
far apart you can get before the sound
gets too faint. Now who didn't make
one of these sets as a child?

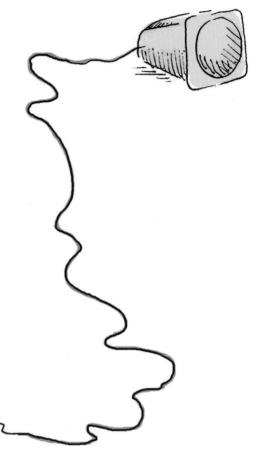

Handy hints...
Choosing a family-friendly campsite

WHAT'S THE STYLE?

Sites with pools, a clubhouse and play areas tend to be busy compared with more tranquil places with the chance to explore the site's natural surroundings. Check out online reviews for advice.

PARENT-FRIENDLY FACILITIES

Has the facilities block got family shower rooms? Many sites offer these plus parent and baby rooms, and most take great pride in the cleanliness of their facilities.

LOCATION, LOCATION, LOCATION

What's on the doorstep? Are you after visitor attractions if the rain clouds roll in, or Mother Nature's playground where you can walk, canoe and cycle whatever the weather?

FAMILY DEALS

Does the campsite give discounts, including single-parent offers?

CALL OF NATURE

If learning more about the local wildlife is important to you, consider pitching up at a Camping in the Forest Site that runs ranger activities.

LOOK FOR AWARDS

Has the site won an AA Caravan and Camping Award, judged by impartial campsite inspectors? It might swing your decision.

THE BARE ESSENTIALS

If you want to light a campfire, ensure you've booked on to a site that allows it. Need to launch your canoe or sailing dinghy from the campsite? Best check before booking.

GO GLAMPING

Tipis and yurts have been springing up across the nation. It's called 'glamping' (glamorous camping, see page 34) and you'll have some home luxuries to hand while still enjoying a closer-to-nature holiday. Ready Camp are popular pre-pitched safari tents on selected Camping and Caravanning Club Sites that offer a great way to get you started without first buying the kit.

Early rising

55
A different light

If you're having breakfast on the campsite, head off for a short family stroll. The wind is often still at this time of day and you'll see your surroundings in a different light, especially if an atmospheric early morning mist is cloaking the ground. Go quietly and see if anyone can identify the surrounding sounds.

56
See the sun rise over water

If camping near water, whether it's the sea on the east coast or a tranquil, tree-fringed lake, pick your spot the night before. Get there nice and early and await one of nature's loveliest free shows. A sunrise is beautiful at any location, but as it lifts itself above the shimmering sea or lakes, the colours dance across the water to enhance the spectacle. Bliss.

57
That first brew of tea

Even if it's chilly, wrap up warm and sit outside as your morning cuppas steam in the cold air. Sit quietly and savour the moment. Look around you and listen out for fellow early risers from the animal kingdom. Be patient (that's where the tea comes in), and local creatures will inquisitively come to you.

58

Guided walks

The RSPB organises guided walks, often with breakfast included. See if you can identify birds through their song or spot them in the trees and bushes. Wrap up warm, take a flask, and remember your bird book and binoculars, or download a bird song recognition app for your smartphone. Late April to early June is a good time of year to appreciate the dawn chorus at its finest.

59

Save the date

Make a note in your diary of International Dawn Chorus day, which is held on the first Sunday in May, and join in. It has been developing for three decades, but with the advent of the internet and social media it has grown rapidly in recent years around the world.

> "Courtesy is infectious and no one has a finer chance of spreading it through the countryside than the hiker."
>
> *Campcraft for Girl Guides*, 1953

60

Seek out the exotic

For something a little different, pitch up at a campsite next door to a safari park or aviary. The dawn chorus you experience will be much more exotic.

Boot camp

61

Rewards and distractions

There are many ways to make a walk interesting for little legs and inquisitive minds, not forgetting Mum and Dad too. Give the walk a purpose, make it fun, use prizes – and the countryside is your oyster.

62

Play games along the way

Help motivate the kids by playing a wildlife word association game. Or even an I-spy countryside special – it's much more interesting than playing it on a motorway.

63

Go treasure hunting

Bags of chocolate coins or wrapped mini eggs are ideal for this. While Dad distracts the children, Mum sneaks ahead to plant a cache of 'treasure' in a tree trunk or other suitable spot. As soon as the kids discover the first cache, they will be swarming over the path looking for the next big find. Ensure there's a steady flow of treasure to keep their interest.

64

Play Hide and Seek

It will be vastly different to the same game played at home and can be on a much grander scale too.

65

Chat about the countryside

It's all around you, so make the most of it. Look for sycamore seeds and fly them as helicopters. Collect feathers to identify the birds they came from when you're back at camp. Seek out strange faces in tree bark.

66

Plan an interesting route

Follow a fun trail with lots to see and explore. Think bridges, waterfalls, stepping-stones and ancient ruins.

67

Mine's a pint

Yes, ice creams are fab but a pitstop at a great British pub is a reward for Mum and Dad, especially at the end of a long route. But it's not all one-way traffic – a bottle of pop and a bag of crisps in the pub garden go a long way with little ones too.

"Achievement and enjoyment are the main aims of all good hiking expeditions."

Campcraft for Girl Guides, 1953

68
Trails with tales

A walk in the countryside becomes something far more exciting when a theme is added. There are plenty of country parks that offer themed forest trails, so remember to pick up a map from the visitor centre as soon as you arrive and add an extra element to your visit.

69
Myths and legends

Kids love stories, so choose an area or trail rich in folklore. Hills and mountains go hand-in-hand with legends, so read up on one in advance and look for clues along the way, reconstructing it as you go.

70
Dream up your own story

As you walk, take it in turns to bring the tale to life. Is that a hungry troll I see under the bridge? Find mushrooms and tell a story about fairies. Crampon scratches on rocks were obviously made by the talons of dragons…

71
Get arty

Take to a trail where there are forest sculptures to enjoy. Some parks have woodland instruments to play along the way too.

72
Book your place

Literature is crammed with real countryside settings. Visit the literary landscape of your favourite book and take a stroll through its pages.

73
Spot a chalk hill drawing

There are many around the country and the best way to see them is on foot. The county of Wiltshire alone has eight chalk horse drawings, each with its own fascinating history.

74

Have a hair-raising hike

The Lake District is criss-crossed by 'corpse roads' once used by isolated communities to take coffins to burial grounds from their remote villages. Unsurprisingly they are the stuff of spooky stories.

75

Sign up for a walking festival

They're a great place to get the walking bug. Walking festivals offer interesting talks, guided walks and the chance to check out the latest outdoors kit and clothing.

76

Walk a waterfall trail

Bad weather can be the camper's bane. The upside is that a waterfall is far more dramatic after a spot of rain. Many trails lead to waterfalls: you'll usually hear them from a distance and they're always worth the walk.

77

In it for the long-haul

Trekking long-distance paths has been growing in popularity. Grab a backpack with all your camping kit and get hiking. There will be plenty of campsites along the way. Don't feel you have to complete an entire walk in one go. Dip in and out of sections and complete the whole route over a longer period of time.

78

Beasties and butterflies

Look towards your feet on a bug hunt or search the skies to spot butterflies. Walking makes us slow down and appreciate our surroundings, so use that time to spot insects. And remember to take the bug-hunting kit.

79

Disused railway trails

These can have great accessibility, are flat and quickly transport you into the countryside away from roads. Look out for the relics of rail travel from yesteryear along the way.

Handy hints...

Make your own trail mix

Trail mix is an ideal snack for walkers to graze on, giving welcome bursts of energy and raising spirits when the going gets tough. Yes, you can buy bags of it but it's much more fun for kids to make their own. What's more, each person can make it to suit his or her own tastebuds. Here's what to consider for a trail mix:

DRIED FRUITS
Dates, raisins, apricots, sliced banana and cranberries.

NUTS
A crunchy mixture including almonds, cashews, walnuts and brazils.

SEEDS
Sunflower, pumpkin and sesame seeds give great flavour and texture.

SWEET STUFF
Break up a chocolate bar or grab a handful of chocolate chips or buttons and mix in with the healthy stuff.

FOR THE LITTLE ONES
Add a cupful of their favourite cereal.

FABULOUS FLAPJACKS
Flapjacks combine complex carbohydrates in the form of oats for a slow release of energy while the sugar and syrup, which are simple carbs, give instant energy. Get the children to bake some at home and experiment with extra ingredients such as dried fruit and chocolate chips. I prefer not to eat them in one go, instead breaking off pieces to enjoy as occasional little pick-me-ups.

Things to remember...

Before you embark on a long family walk, make sure you've got the right clothing and footwear for everyone and get the kids involved with route planning and picnic prepping.

ADVENTURE TIME
Tell the children you're going on an adventure, not a walk – they're much more likely to enjoy it.

PACK THE SNACKS
Take snacks and plenty to drink (we all hate being thirsty). Water is also useful for washing little hands along the way.

SLIP SLOP SLAP
Remember to pack wet wipes, sun cream and hats.

TAKE THINGS TO DO
There's the camera, binoculars, butterfly net, bug pots...

PREPARE A PLAN B
If the weather turns bad on a walk, don't push on regardless – it could put them off next time.

PUDDLES ARE FUN
Make a big splash or launch a leaf.

PICK UP STICKS
Sticks are Mother Nature's way of saying help yourself to a free multi-purpose toy. Be sure to find yourself a good one.

PRACTICE MAKES PERFECT
Don't expect everyone to suddenly be capable of a big hike. Build up to it – you'll all enjoy it more.

80
Lay a trail

A fun activity for the family starts by splitting into two groups. The first group lays a trail that will be followed by the second. Then swap roles. Bet you get lost, albeit briefly. Sticks and stones can be used to make arrows pointing the way and they can be laid on the ground or higher up on fallen tree trunks or smaller plants. Clumps of long grass can be tied into knots while still left in the ground, with the shorter section at the top pointing in the direction of the trail.

Wool can be tied to low tree branches or on hedges and gates to mark a path – just don't forget to collect it up again. If younger children are taking part, try to keep the distance between pointers equal, perhaps at an agreed number of paces.

Add an element of confusion to the trail by laying it in a clear direction then doubling back for a while, or lay a false track by making a circle that brings them back to the same spot.

81

Lay a cypher trail

A stroll through the countryside becomes much more exciting if there's a story or game involved. And by using cyphers – codes – youngsters can add an element of mystery and intrigue by playing the roles of secret agents. Unravel the cypher trail to locate a hidden cache, such as a hole in a tree where they will find secret plans or even treasure (chocolate works well). The trail can only be followed by the person who devised the code and their fellow secret agents who know how to decipher it.

Devise a cypher strip containing symbols that provide the directions for the trail. A triangle, for example, means turn left, while a square means turn right. A circle of stones could mean take 10 paces along the path to find the next clue. A symbol could

be created to denote a tree or other features such as branches or rocks.

Alternatively, devise a code using symbols to represent the alphabet. So A could be represented by three wavy lines, while a B is a square with a cross inside. The directions – "turn right at the rotten oak tree" – are then encyphered using the symbols and the secret agent has to decipher each instruction with a crib sheet. Once the cypher has been created, draw a basic map of the area including landmarks and mark the cyphers at corresponding points. The symbols can also be repeated on the ground at the same points of the map, perhaps scratched into dusty ground.

At the end the kids will have drawn a map, devised a cypher and decoded it to follow a trail that led to a secret cache. It's a mini adventure and learning experience all in one that can be enjoyed in one go or over a period of time.

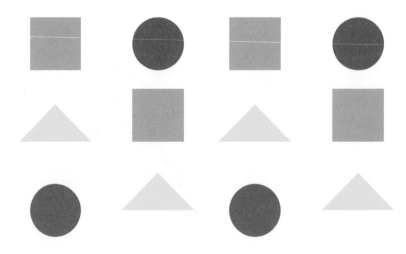

82
Let the kids lead the expedition

Here's a simple idea that works best in a country park with well-marked paths. To help develop navigation and decision-making skills, put the children in charge, give them the map and let them decide the way to go whenever you reach a junction. Help them by pointing out the most obvious features on the map and then on the ground once they spot them – it's an engaging and visual way to learn.

Alternatively, follow a zigzag route by alternating between taking the left-hand or right-hand path. Or flip a coin at each junction: heads we go left, tails we branch right. At the end of the walk use a map, whether locally produced by the park or your own, to work out the route you've just taken. Start by re-orientating yourself to work out where you are. Look for a landmark close to where you're standing, such as a visitor centre or car park, find it on the map and then use the map to work out your route. Highlighter pens are great to mark out routes in advance to make them easier to follow or once complete. Why not get the kids to pause and draw a pictorial map of their surroundings as they walk?

83
Lay a rope trail

Tie a long piece of rope to a tree and use it to create a trail around and over small obstacles. Each participant is blindfolded and must then use their hands to carefully follow the trail from start to finish. Onlookers can help with clues as to where the rope goes next and what obstacles are in the way.

84
Lay a scent trail

This is an old Scout game in which the trail-maker rubs half an onion on things such as tree trunks, gateposts and rocks at various points along the trail. The others in the party then find out how difficult it is to follow the scent using just the sense of smell. Try adding a blindfold (using someone to act as a guide along the trail) to find out whether the loss of sight heightens the sense of smell.

Things to remember...

FINDING FOOTPRINTS
Certain weather conditions and seasons make it easier to spot footprints, so this is an ideal autumn or winter activity. Wet mud and snow are perfect!

WAIT FOR WINTER
In winter the plants will have died back, which will make it much easier to spot clues.

85
Learn tracking skills

You can really hone your outdoor skills by learning to track wildlife. The best starting place is to sign up for one of the ranger-led activity sessions that are held across the country and include some night-time walks when the wildlife will be quite different from that you'd find during daylight hours. Rangers have a wealth of knowledge about the local wildlife to share and teach tracking skills.

It's exciting to spot an animal track in the ground, identify the creature and follow its path. Often it will lead to a waterhole, where other animal footprints are likely to be found. Although you may not get sight of the creature itself, it's still rewarding to be able to identify the telltale signs that an animal has recently been on the same track as you.

86
Look for footprints

Deer have hooves split into two (cloven). Foxes have four toes above a pad and can be mistaken for dog tracks, so look for footprints that are narrow and diamond-shaped. Otters have five toes with a large pad and in soft ground they can show webs and claws. Badgers also have five toes plus long claws on the front feet.

87
Poo gives a clue

Droppings will help identify local wildlife and their behaviour. Rabbit poo is a common one to spot and looks like little clusters of round balls. Badgers use droppings to mark their territory and deposit it in dung pits (mini latrines, if you like). If you poke some types of poo with a stick it may reveal the animal's dinner, for example fish bones and scales in otter poo, which is called spraint. Hedgehog droppings are shiny, black and about 5cm long, while fox poo looks slimy and stinks, as many dog owners will know, because our four-legged friends love rolling in it.

88
Fur snags

It's not unusual to spot a wire fence covered in sheep wool but there are other creatures that will also snag their fur on trees or brambles. Learn an animal's colour and type of fur and see if you can spot some.

89
Signs of activity

Some creatures will nibble at tree bark for food. Deer strip it vertically, unlike other animals. Badgers create the wonderfully named snuffle holes when digging for food. Try not to mix them up with rabbit scrapes, which cause golfers problems.

90
Home time

Countryside walks will often lead to the discovery of an animal's home. Learn how to identify them, for example by looking for nearby tracks or droppings, and learn their names. Rabbits live in warrens, foxes have dens that are also called earths, and badgers dig setts.

Weather-watching

91

What's in a name?

Try remembering (and pronouncing) the 10 main types of cloud, called *genera*, which are grouped into three height categories.

High clouds
Cirrus
Cirrocumulus
Cirrostratus

Medium clouds
Altocumulus
Altostratus
Nimbostratus

Low clouds
Stratocumulus
Stratus
Cumulus
Cumulonimbus

Cirrus are high clouds. The Latin name means locks or tufts of hair – and that's a bit like how they look. Cirrus clouds suggest there's a change of weather on the way. Who's going to tighten the tent's guy lines then?

Stratus clouds can produce light drizzle and are low level, often the reason for overcast days. If low enough they hug the ground in the form of fog or mist.

Cumulus clouds, common on sunny days, are often called fair-weather clouds. They are fluffy-looking but they can develop into cumulonimbus or cumulus congestus, bringing showers, the camper's nightmare.

"Weather, which at home is merely a conversational topic of tepid interest, becomes in camp a most important factor. A little weather wisdom may save a deal of work and worry."

Campcraft for Girl Guides, 1953

92

Learn to identify clouds

Clouds are formed when heat causes water from sources such as lakes, oceans and rivers to evaporate. The moist air rises, expands and cools, creating small droplets of water that form into clouds. For a cloud to form it needs certain conditions – the right temperature and something to hold onto, like particles of smoke or dust.

Once the droplets are big enough they fall back to earth, into the waterways and seas – not forgetting our tents and caravans – and the whole cycle gets underway again. Identifying clouds is fun and gives clues as to what weather could be on the way.

93

A face in the clouds

Next time you're out for a family walk in the countryside, find a dry patch of ground, lie down and look up at the clouds. Then spot, describe and point out faces and other interesting shapes

and colours. Cumulus clouds are often described as looking like cauliflowers. Can you spot other vegetable shapes? Get everyone's imagination going by making up stories about stratus, cirrus and their mates and get really fluffy with your descriptions.

94

Take a time-lapse

The movement of clouds across the sky adds to their fascination. Use a smartphone to make a time-lapse video of how they shift across the sky.

95

Spot a special cloud

Orographic clouds are types made or affected by land (hills and mountains), and a banner cloud is created by a mountain basically getting in the way. The wind is forced up the mountain, the water vapour condenses and forms a cloud. The lower pressure on the leeward side of the mountain (the side sheltered from the wind) then creates the banner shape. Switzerland's famously beautiful mountain, the Matterhorn, regularly provides Alpine spectators with a classic example of a banner cloud.

Mother Nature is not responsible for every type of cloud. A condensation trail is a distinctive straight line high across the sky caused by a jet aircraft ejecting water vapour from its exhaust. A 'contrail' will only be created if the air outside the plane is both moist and cold – freezing in fact. On a clear day contrails can be seen criss-crossing the sky.

96
Count the seconds

Want to work out how far away a lightning strike was? Begin counting the seconds after spotting the lightning, stop when you hear the crack of thunder and divide the number by five. So if you counted to 10, the lightning strike was about two miles away.

97
Make a rainbow...

Rainbows are multi-coloured arcs caused by sunlight reflecting, refracting and dispersing through raindrops. And you can create your own. You need a hosepipe and a sunny day. Simply turn the nozzle on to a fine mist setting, or hold your thumb over the end of the pipe to create one, and aim it in the direction of your shadow. The angle may need to be adjusted but a rainbow should appear. Kids can then draw what they've just created using lots of bright colours, not forgetting the pot of gold at the end.

98
... or spot a moonbow

Rainbows can also appear at night, though are seldom seen, and are called moonbows or lunar rainbows. The amazing thing about a moonbow, which often appears white, is that the light comes from the sun 93 million miles away, reflects off the moon and then heads a mere 238,900 miles to the earth. The best chance of seeing one is near a waterfall, thanks to the spray. Maybe one to look out for on a night hike.

Handy hints...
Special natural effects to spot

CREPUSCULAR RAYS

These are beams of sunlight that appear to radiate from the sun, though in fact they are almost parallel and shine through gaps in the cloud. One version often seen is Jacob's Ladder, which shines downwards in beams of light contrasting against patches of cloud shadow.

HALO

This is a circle of light around the moon or sun caused by tiny ice crystals in cirrus or cirrostratus clouds through which light reflects or refracts to make faint rainbow colours. The saying (with variations) 'when halo rings moon or sun, rain's approaching on the run' suggests wet weather's on the way, so get the brollies ready. You may well have seen a halo closer to the ground in particularly cold weather, as they can form around bright lights such as streetlamps, an effect caused by tiny ice crystals ('diamond dust').

GLORY

The next time you have a window seat in a plane, look out for a 'glory', which can often be spotted from aircraft. The sun needs to be directly behind your head while a cloud must be directly in front of you. The shadow of the plane that appears will be circled by multi-coloured rings – a glorious sight to behold.

BROCKEN SPECTRES

As the name suggests, Brocken spectres are somewhat spookier than glories and are associated with hills and mountains. They are glories that create a halo around your shadow that only you can see. A person standing beside you would only see their own Brocken spectre. The sun needs to be low and behind you and you must be higher than the cloud or mist. It's certainly a spooky phenomenon to spot on a misty mountain.

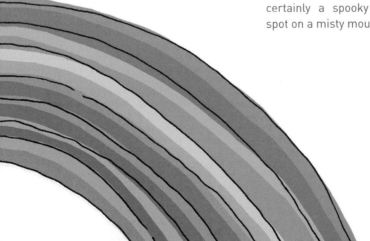

....

"Damp comes to the camper in a variety of ways. For instance he may get damp by not having his waterproofs at the time he needs them. He may, of course, be a reckless fellow, and not bother himself about such things."

Thomas Hiram Holding

Author of *The Campers' Handbook,* published in 1908, and founder of The Camping and Caravanning Club

....

99

Make your own campsite weather station

Recording the weather is great to do while on a camping holiday, since you'll be much more aware of the weather around you. Try to capture a range of information and put some of the old rhymes to the test.

1. Start the weather station with some pine cones. An open cone suggests fine weather, as the cone wants its seeds to disperse but rain may be on the way if it closes to protect them.

2. Following a trip to the beach, pin up some seaweed in a sheltered spot. Seaweed absorbs atmospheric moisture, so if the air is humid, the seaweed will be moist and bad weather could be coming your way. If it's dry, the weather may be fine.

3. Use sticky tack to attach a thermometer to the inside back of a white box. Place the box in some shade, protected from direct weather conditions (outside the tent or caravan)

with the thermometer upright, and head back at specific times of day to record the temperature. If the car is nearby, compare it to the reading on the dashboard.

4. Make a rain gauge by cutting a two-litre plastic water bottle about a third of the way down (where the bottle's diameter becomes consistent). Take the top part (without the lid) and invert it into the top of the lower section and fix it in place with paperclips or tape. Mark a scale in centimetres on the side of the bottle. Secure it level to the ground with sand, mud or stones to avoid it blowing over. Then place the gauge in an unsheltered spot. Each day, measure the contents at the same time and note down the results before emptying it.

5. Find a spot where wild marigolds are growing. If they're open wide, it's in anticipation of fine weather, but closed up suggests a downpour.

6. Lastly, make a weather chart to record all your findings and perhaps devise some symbols to note information such as the day's weather and types of clouds.

Handy hints...
Help from Mother Nature

What do the weather rhymes mean?

WEATHER PROPHETS
Learning Mother Nature's own weather forecasting methods is a cool way of passing knowledge down the generations. The rhymes we learned as children are just as relevant today although, that said, I cannot vouch that there is any scientific substance to them. Kids will still love testing them out though!

BIRDS
Rooks remain near their roosts in unsettled weather and birds preen their feathers before rain. Birds flying high in the sky is a good sign, hence the phrase 'swallows high, stay dry, swallows low, wet will blow'.

COWS
Cows turn their tails to the wind when it's going to rain – who wouldn't turn their backs to a cold blast? Does lying down mean the same thing? Many think not.

RABBITS
Bunnies tuck into their food early before a wet night, apparently.

DEER AND CATTLE
Both move off hills and mountains when they sense bad weather. Maybe it's time to cut short that hill walk...

THE REDDISH MOON HAS WATER IN HER EYE, BEFORE TOO LONG YOU WON'T BE DRY
Could a low-pressure front be pushing in dust to create the red colour of the moon, resulting in unsettled weather?

RAIN BEFORE 7, FINE BY 11
As Britain is such a small country, its weather moves quickly with the help of the westerly flow off the Atlantic. Though it may seem like a low-pressure front has been seen off in the morning, it's not always the case – and the rain keeps on coming.

RED SKY AT NIGHT, SHEPHERD'S DELIGHT, RED SKY IN THE MORNING, SHEPHERD'S WARNING
The low setting or rising sun projects red rays and lots of clouds are needed to give the colour effect. Red rays at sunset can often mean fair weather's on the way due to high pressure. Likewise, if the red sky is in the morning that high pressure is likely to have moved on and there's low pressure behind it bringing wind and rain. Wellies at the ready then.

WHEN SHEEP GATHER IN A HUDDLE, TOMORROW WILL HAVE A PUDDLE
Are they really aware that rain is on the way and herding together for shelter? Or are they just trying to pull the wool over our eyes?

Mindfulness and Yoga

100
Learn a basic breathing technique

The Hakini Mudra in yoga is said to help boost thinking and concentration, and can be easily practised anywhere. Hold up your hands in front of your chest, palms facing each other, but not touching. Bring the fingertips of your right hand towards the fingertips of your left hand so that they are touching. Move your gaze upwards. Inhale while placing your tongue against the roof of your mouth. Then exhale while allowing your tongue to relax. Practise these steps several times. It's helpful when you've forgotten something momentarily and want to recollect it.

101
Use the clouds or the stars

Breath awareness can also be practised lying on your back and focusing on the clouds. Just watch them move across the sky as you breathe in and out. This almost becomes a mini-meditation as the mind focuses on the clouds and not on worries or the constant chit-chat in our minds. Try staying like this for anything from two to 15 minutes. Alternatively, focus on the stars in the night sky to relax body and mind.

"A sound camp is as good a tonic to the mind as to the body. The change of scene – often from drab and limited surroundings to the beauty and spaciousness of the country; the novelty of living in the open with its different sights and sounds... all these things create a background built up of memories which will live on long after camping days are over."

Campcraft for Girl Guides, 1953

Handy hints...
Five steps to mental wellbeing

1. CONNECT
Spend time developing relationships with friends and family. Stay connected. Campsites are sociable places to do just that.

2. BE ACTIVE
It can be as simple as going for a country walk or taking up a new activity such as canoeing or sailing and making it part of family life.

3. KEEP LEARNING
Developing new skills helps build confidence and provides a sense of achievement. Learn how to navigate and feel that sense of achievement when you successfully enjoy a day out in the hills with map and compass.

4. GIVE TO OTHERS
Small acts of kindness will put a smile on your face and that of others too. Larger acts, such as voluntary work, provide a greater feeling of giving to others. The Camping and Caravanning Club has a Countryside Care group that combines camping with voluntary work to look after the environment around campsites. It's smiles all round then.

5. BE MINDFUL
Be in the moment. Take notice of your thoughts, feelings and the physical world around you. And start now.

102
Sun Salutation

Who's up for an early start and a good morning stretch following a night under canvas? Unzip the tent, put a towel or mat on the grass and feel the warmth on your body as you do the Sun Salutation (*Surya Namaskar*).

1. Start with the Mountain pose by pushing down firmly on the ground with the feet, palms together in front of the chest.
2. Inhale and push your arms (hands together) towards the sky, looking up.
3. Breathe out and fold your body forward, hands touching the ground.
4. Then move into a lunge by bending knees (if necessary) and, with an inhale, step back with your left leg, keeping fingers touching the floor.
5. Breath out and move your right leg back to join the left leg, forming a Plank pose (in effect the starting position of a press up).
6. Continue to exhale, and lower your body down so your elbow forms a right angle and your body is about 5cm off the ground.

Move smoothly through each pose and repeat the sequence by changing the leg that you step back on during the lunge.

The Sun Salutation is a warming, calming start to the day. You could also do the Moon Salutation when the sun has gone to bed.

Handy hints...
Three elements of a balanced yoga practice

1. BREATH AWARENESS
Listen and connect to your breath. Where better to do this than sitting quietly watching the sun rise or beneath the twinkling stars?

2. POSTURE
Yoga involves gently moving and stretching the body into various shapes to work all parts of the body, keeping joints active and supple while also stretching and strengthening the muscles. By performing the postures (*asanas*) the body becomes comfortably tired and satisfied, ready to rest quietly, and is more likely to remain still during the meditation and mindfulness practice.

3. MEDITATION, MINDFULNESS AND RELAXATION
This is used to quieten and calm the mind. That means the body can relax and rejuvenate at the same time.

103
Become a Tree, a Soaring Bird and an Eagle

Many yoga poses have animal names and can be combined in a sequence complete with actions and sounds that will appeal to vivid young imaginations. Here's a sequence that also lends itself to inventing a fun story to accompany it.

Stand firm on the right leg, rooting down into the earth. After holding and breathing for a few seconds, begin to let the branches of the Tree (your arms) sway in the breeze and make rustling noises to imitate leaves, all the time trying to stand firm and strong through your foot into the earth like roots. Raise your arms straight above your head, hands separate but palms facing, then join palms together and sway some more, all the time making rustling noises.

Then a large bird flies out of the Tree. As you take your arms out to the side, place both feet on floor and flap your arms up and down as you bend your knees and simultaneously bounce up and down, synchronising with arms, like a bird in flight – the Soaring Bird.

The Soaring Bird then transforms into the Eagle by bending the right knee and wrapping the leg around the left one. Then wrap your arms by placing the left over the right and wrap the wrists around each other, bringing together the palms. Let the Eagle lean forward a little as if scanning the ground from a height, and hold the pose for a few seconds.

Repeat the sequence, changing the Tree to standing on the left leg.

Things to remember...

WARM UP FIRST
Yoga is just like any exercise. You need to warm up muscles and joints beforehand. And remember to rest between poses too.

START WITH A CLASS
It's a good idea to learn the poses and breathing techniques at a class. Although yoga injuries are uncommon, it makes sense to learn from a qualified instructor and choose the level of class that best suits you.

TAKE IT SLOWLY
Don't be tempted to move onto the more challenging poses until both children and parents have more confidence. Also bear in mind that kids are less aware of their physical limitations than grown-ups so don't let them get carried away. There are many breathing techniques and it's important to learn them properly, especially for children whose lungs are still developing. Meditation is also something that is best learned from an expert.

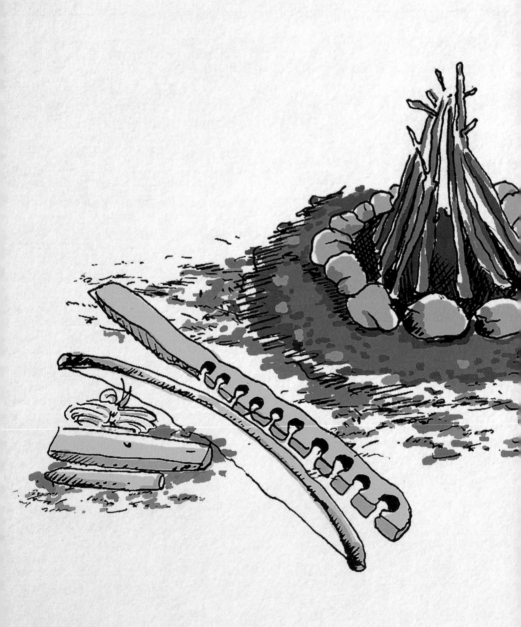

3
RELEARNING
ANCIENT SKILLS

"Our houses are such unwieldy property that we are often imprisoned rather than housed in them."

Henry David Thoreau
Walden, 1854

Camping together as a family can provide unrivalled opportunities for outdoor adventure and, just for a week or two, the chance to challenge ourselves to embrace a simpler, more natural lifestyle in which ancient skills and survival techniques play a part. It's an ideal time to pass on some of the fundamental life skills that were once handed down through the generations as a matter of course but in recent years have been usurped by technology, tablets and smartphones.

Building a den

Forests and woods are really fun places and it's amazing how, throughout the generations, the first thing that children of all ages want to do once they start exploring is make a den. Their determination to create shelter in the 'wilderness' by dragging hefty fallen branches and lugging big piles of sticks across a considerable distance to their chosen location may be the response to some deeply primitive home-making urge.

Den-building is a great activity to get kids visualising and planning their structure, experimenting with different designs for stability, improvising with natural materials and learning how to increase a shelter's strength. Then they must consider how best to insulate it with foliage to keep the warmth in and the rain out. This is where it helps to learn about the different qualities of wood and forest plants, not to mention the idiosyncracies of the weather and how to read them. The den will protect you better from the elements if in turn you have built it in a sheltered spot.

The primitive urge to create a home continues once a basic shelter has been established – whether it's a tipi made of sticks or a glamped-up modern tent with all mod cons.

The wonder of wood

Woodcraft is both fun and practical – and with some newly made furniture on display you'll be bringing a classic retro feel to camp as well as adding to your creature comforts. However, there's much more to it than that. Learning about different trees and their qualities is important to ensure that you choose the best wood for the job and use it correctly.

Non-toxic wood such as willow, hazel and sycamore should be used for cooking utensils. Damp wood ash makes an effective natural scourer for pots and pans with the help of a cloth and a little elbow grease. Willow is great for construction, as is oak, which also burns hot and long, while elm smokes profusely. Many trees are considered to have medicinal properties too.

Getting to know our trees helps reconnect us and younger generations with nature. Learning through experience is a great way for knowledge to be retained and hopefully shared again one day with tomorrow's generations. Having fun making woodcraft furniture is just the start. You've already gathered the sticks so why not set the family a woodcraft challenge? Then award a prize for the best (they don't have to do the washing up using their new washstand, page 93). Before you start, remember to get knotted by practising your rope skills – the two go hand in hand.

"When we leave behind us the conventions of civilisation we are faced again with the same primitive necessities, and woodcraft becomes, once more, the only key to living comfortably out of doors."

Campcraft for Girl Guides, 1953

Tied up in knots

Learning to lace up our shoes is, for most of us, our first exposure to the art of tying knots. However, these days that experience comes much later in childhood thanks to the widespread use of easy-fasten shoes. Today's children seem more waist-high than knee-high when they master the shoelace knot.

Learning how to tie knots is not only an important part of camp life, it can be great fun too. It's useful, and in some situations essential, to know which knot to use and when – and to tie it correctly. Good rope skills mean you also know how to untie the knot. I once went sailing with a former England rugby player who tried to untie a knot that had been put under huge tension. Despite his hands being the size of hams it took him the best part of half an hour to pull the knot apart. I'll give credit where it's due. It took some considerable strength and patience to sort out the rope.

Many people learned knots in the Scouts or Guides and no doubt had a moment of panic when asked to tie the knot for the flagpole. And how many of us hoped we'd correctly tied a reef knot rather than a granny knot, the latter being similarly tied but of little use?

Knots are an essential part of many great outdoor activities such as sailing, canoeing and climbing, not to mention key when making field repairs to tents and awnings. You need to rely on your knots if you're hanging from two trees in a hammock, and feel confident the tarpaulin ('tarp') you've just rigged as a shelter isn't going to blow away in the wind. And if a guy line breaks in the middle of a wet and windy night, it's best to be able to fix it quickly. That's where knots come in.

Building a campfire

A bushcraft expert once told me: "Ninety per cent of successful fire lighting is in the preparation." Having tried it myself on many occasions and in different ways, he's absolutely correct. Get the small detail right and you significantly improve your chances of success. I would even go so far as to say fire lighting is an art. However, it's one of those skills from which people seem to be getting increasingly disconnected. After all, how many parents can say they have taught their children how to how to build, light, maintain and extinguish a fire these days? Or even how to safely strike a match? There's something special about a campfire. Yes, it's a place of warmth and somewhere to cook but it's so much more than that. A campfire becomes the centrepiece of a sociable camping evening where people chat and enjoy each other's company, and even sing rounds or tell a few tales of outdoor adventures. Neighbours get invited over to join in.

The feeling of achievement when a fire is lit, especially without the assistance of a match or lighter, is significant. It feels like a small triumph over the elements. If it's cold and wet it's a major victory. Thankfully campfires are making a bit of a comeback and are something all the family can enjoy.

Campfire cooking is a great way to feel connected to the countryside. You have to work to build the fire, light it and keep it going. Cooking tasty yet simple food is your reward. When there's a group of you, campfire cooking is incredibly sociable and perhaps the highlight of the day. The campfire takes centre stage, providing warmth and light, while the cooking and food fan the flames of the occasion. Mix in some conversation, storytelling and a few songs afterwards and you have the recipe for a fantastic time.

Campfire storytelling

It seems that ever since people mastered the control of fire they used the campfire as a setting in which to tell stories. This aspect of ancient history somehow transcended different cultures and civilisations around the planet.

Fire meant cooked food, warmth, companionship, security from wild animals, and a longer day once the sun had set. It drew people together and was the ideal setting

for one of the earliest and most basic forms of entertainment – storytelling. It was a time and a way to pass down tales of family or tribal deeds to future generations, and no doubt embellish them along the way. Tales would become legends.

Today the draw of the campfire is still an atmospheric focal point around which to share stories. It creates a natural circle for sitting as well as creating its own light, noise and smell. The storytelling tips that follow will work without a campfire, though there's no doubt a flickering flame and the crackle of burning wood will add to the occasion.

Campfire singalong

Musical entertainment combined with a campfire is perhaps as old as man's ability to light and control the fire. Yet in today's society we are constantly entertained, not in a spontaneous, communal way, but by electronic devices that allow us to tap into instant entertainment whenever we feel like it. Young people have a high level of expectation that entertainment will be provided for them – it's at their fingertips and they just have to switch on or plug in.

Having a campfire singalong is learning once more how to create our own entertainment. Singing brings people closer together and provides a sense of achievement when it works. It can also have you in fits of laughter when it doesn't. It's good for the soul.

Most people, young and old, love to sing, as witnessed by the many choirs and singing groups popping up all over the country. Why not take a musical trip down memory lane and enjoy a selection of nostalgic songs to sing around the campfire? It's also a good opportunity to keep alive traditional British folk songs.

Many of us will remember campfire songs learned as Scouts or Guides, and even the smallest mention of one brings the tune and the words flooding back, such as the classic campfire song *Kumbaya*. So get toasting another delicious s'more (see page 194) and have a harmonious time enjoying a campsite singsong.

Den-building

104

Build a tipi

A tipi-shaped den is perhaps the most common den structure and the easiest to construct. To make one that leans against the base of a tree, find some large branches of similar size and place them around the tree trunk or part of it (ideally, choose a tree with a trunk that is not too wide). Overlap and interlock the branches at the top for added stability and then weave some smaller branches horizontally between the main supports. By starting at the bottom and working up, there will always be a lower level to support the new layer you are making. On top of this frame place piles of leaves and twigs and continue to weave longer sticks into the frame to make a protective lattice.

You could also build a freestanding tipi away from a tree by ensuring that the main supporting branches are well interlocked and by tying them securely together at the top where they connect.

105

Open-fronted den

Find two sturdy branches with a Y-shaped fork at the top and drive them firmly into the ground roughly a couple of metres apart. Place another strong branch across the top of the two branches to form a ridge pole.

Lean more branches against the ridge pole to create a lean-to structure and push the base of the branches into the ground a little for added stability. If you have some cord, tie them at the top. Weaving long, thin branches horizontally across the lean-to roof will create a lattice effect that will be easy to cover with leaves, twigs, and large pieces of bark, plus branches that still have some twigs and leaves attached.

Work from the bottom up, overlapping in the same way as tiles on a roof to allow any rain to drain downwards rather than drip inwards.

For added protection from the weather, build sides at either end adopting the same technique as used for the roof (though with less of an angle) and again add insulation.

106

The A-frame

This den is also the basis for a classic-style tent. Create the same initial structure as the open-fronted den using two forked branches and a ridge pole. Then add additional branches for a lean-to roof, but on both sides, and insulate again.

107

Time for a 'tarp'

Introduce a simple tarpaulin, or tarp, and den-building options expand dramatically, as does the ability to make them much more waterproof.

Tarps are versatile pieces of camping kit that can easily be tied to trees and bushes to add extra protection from the elements. The simplest use is to drape a tarp around the den and securely tie it to the structure or peg it down. Branches make the supports with the tarp providing the shelter. Instead of building a lean-to roof as with the open-fronted and A-frame dens, build the initial structure using the three branches and then tie the tarp across the ridge pole, pegging out the corners. Depending on the size of the tarp, it can effectively make a ridge tent or form an open-fronted shelter.

108

Peg it out

Tarps can be pitched in a variety of ways that mean you don't have to use branches and sticks to build a shelter – you can simply tie it to one or more trees and peg it out. In fact they're so versatile that when you've finished using it with the den, it can be thrown over equipment that's being packed away to protect it from rain, used as a temporary groundsheet to keep kit off a wet and muddy ground, or even strung up to make an improvised badminton net. Every camping family should have one.

Things to remember...

FORAGE FOR WOOD
Use only felled or fallen branches for den-building.

FIRE AWAY
Never attempt to light a fire inside a den. If you have permission from the landowner, you could build a fire pit outside it (see page 103).

HAMMOCK-STYLE TENTS
Many campsites do not allow hammock-type tents to be pitched using trees, so if you're planning this sort of shelter, beneath an A-frame tarp, remember to get the landowner's permission first.

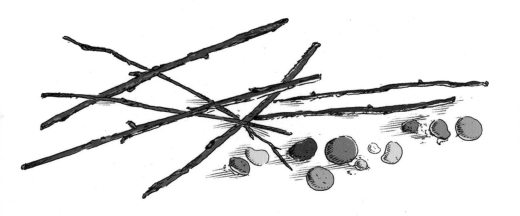

Handy hints...
Building a den

SIT INSIDE
When adding the insulating layer, sit inside the den and look outwards. Light shining through the shelter will help identify the gaps you need to cover up.

JUST HAVE LUNCH
Instead of camping in the den, why not just have a picnic or dinner inside?

MAKE IT COMFY
Think about adding a dry, soft flooring of leaves for added comfort.

THE NEW FOREST
Camping in the Forest, a joint venture between The Camping and Caravanning Club and the Forestry Commission, has a number of sites in the New Forest, which is an excellent location for den-building. There is plenty of woodland and clearings in which to scavenge wood from the forest floor and craft your den. Avoid using bracken and other ferns as they contain carcinogens.

LEAVE IT FOR OTHERS
Once finished with the den, you could leave it standing so that it can be used by other children or inspire them to make their own. If you prefer to dismantle it, leave no trace by scattering the wood.

GO ON A COURSE
Have fun and learn about the forest at the same time by joining a den-building course.

VIDEO YOUR DEN-BUILDING
Many smartphones are able to record time-lapse video footage. Set up the phone in a stable spot, set it to record on time-lapse and later watch how it all came together, branch by branch.

Woodcraft

109

Make your own washstand

Gather three sturdy sticks of equal thickness and length to make a tripod (you want your washing-up bowl at waist height). Lay them side-by-side and, with strong string or cord, wrap around the sticks about two thirds of the way up. Leave enough string to tie a reef knot (see page 99) at the standing end of the string before doing the binding around the three sticks, about 2cm in length.

A 'frap' is a turn made over the lashing (see page 98 for knotty terms) between spars that pulls them tightly together. Use the working end of the chord to do this a couple of times tightly around the spars. Firstly poles 1 and 2, then poles 2 and 3, and lastly 3 and 1.

A reef knot beneath the lashing then secures the tripod. The sticks are opened out to form a tripod and a round washing-up bowl sits neatly in the top section. The washstand can be made more rigid by lashing sticks close to the end of the tripod legs at the top and bottom, as cross beams.

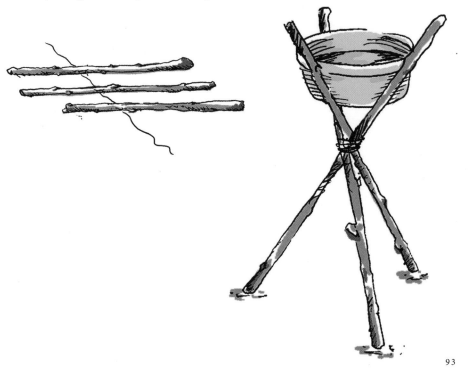

110

Really useful welly pegs

This is an easy way to keep wellies clean, dry and out of the way. Find some strong sticks about double the length of your wellington boot. Sharpen one end to make it easier to push into the ground and trim off any twigs. It needs to be stable in the ground to hold the upturned welly while also keeping it off the ground.

111

Every tent needs a shoe rack

Find four strong sticks that can be driven into the ground, each with branch offshoots that can be trimmed to resemble a Y-shape that points upwards. The two sticks at the rear need to be longer than the front pair, and all four are pushed into the ground. Two more sturdy sticks trimmed of any offshoots act as cross beams that sit on the four sticks in the ground. The heels of the shoes sit on the higher spar, with the toes resting on the lower cross beam.

112

Traditional broom

A besom (a broom made of twigs tied around a stick) is fun to make, can help with the duty rota and, if nothing else, will keep as a prop for next Hallowe'en. Birch twigs are ideal for the brush section, while hazel is well suited to the handle. Otherwise, improvise with what's to hand. Collect a good bundle of long twigs, as straight as possible. Tie strong cord firmly to the handle about 30cm from the bottom with the bulk of it ready to tie to the twigs as the layers build up. Place a selection of twigs around the handle. Then bind them together by coiling the cord around the handle for about 15cm. Continue to build up twig layers until you have a full broom head. Ensure the last set of twigs is securely fastened.

113

Whittle a tent peg

Whittling is a useful skill to learn and can actually be quite relaxing.

"If a person desires to enjoy camping in all weathers he must have a thoroughly efficient equipment."

Thomas Hiram Holding

Author of *The Campers' Handbook*, published in 1908, and founder of The Camping and Caravanning Club

---

It's great to pass the time on a rainy day, and there's the added benefit of having a useful bit of camping kit when you've finished. There is still a place in camping for traditional wooden tent pegs, which are especially suited to holding firm in sandy ground. An improvised wooden peg can also be useful if pitching a tarp for shelter without attaching all guy lines to trees. And if the ground is soft and your own tent pegs are short, you can make a longer peg from wood. If you don't have a mallet, use another larger piece of wood to hammer the peg into the ground.

114

Build a collection

Encourage everyone to make a tent peg from locally foraged wood on each camping trip and build up a collection over time. The pegs are great practical items for pitching your tent but, even better, they also evoke happy memories from previous camping holidays.

115

Make a bushcraft peg

Using a sturdy piece of hazel, a good thumb-width in diameter and about 25cm long, sharpen the end that will be driven into the ground using a forehand grip or chest lever grip on your sheath knife (see pages 96–97). If the peg is too sharp the end will snap off, so ensure it is sufficiently blunt. First, create a V-notch by making a cross near the top of the peg, cut at 45 degrees to the stick, using a stop cut, in other words, pressing down into the wood with the thumb on your least dominant hand on to the back of the knife. Then make a push cut going up to one side of the cross made by the stop cut (due to the cross, the knife will stop at the original cut). A push cut downwards at the top will remove this small piece of wood. Repeat on the other side.

Continue until the desired depth has been achieved, which must be sufficient to hold the guy line but not so deep that the peg will break when hammered.

Handy hints...
Working with wood

GET PERMISSION

Ask the landowner's permission before cutting down any new wood.

BRING SOME BAMBOO

If it's going to be tricky to get sufficient sticks near your campsite, take along a bundle of bamboo canes.

INSTANT KINDLING

Whenever you do any whittling or woodcraft, save any wood shavings to use as kindling for the campfire, keeping them dry, of course.

Things to remember...

LEARN THE CORRECT KNIFE TECHNIQUES

Always choose the right type of knife for the job and treat it with respect. Learn to use the correct grips (below). When using the knife, cut away from your body and know where the knife will land if it should slip. Be aware of your working environment and the people around you, and stop if there's any distraction.

Find a stable surface such as a tree stump to use as a chopping block. Avoid using the knife when it gets dark or if you're tired. It's important to keep the knife in good condition – sharp and well maintained – as dull blades are harder to work with and more likely to slip. For added stability when carving or cutting, sit or kneel down and rest your elbows on your knees.

Whenever you need to pass a knife to another person, point the handle, not the blade, in the direction of the person receiving it (see photo top left, facing page). Make sure that the blade's spine (the blunt part) is sitting on the skin, between thumb and forefinger, with the sharp edge facing upwards.

KNIFE SAFETY

Open and close folding blades and saws very carefully in order to avoid trapping fingers.

Keep the knife sheathed or folded unless in use, and have it on your person or in your pack – don't let it fall into the hands of someone who doesn't know how to use it. Remove and replace it carefully in the sheath by keeping fingers away from the sheath edge closest to the knife's sharp edge. Always keep the knife sheathed and pointing downwards when walking. Know and follow the law in relation to knives.

Safely gripping a sheath knife

FOREHAND GRIP

This is a common, strong grip for powerful cuts (see photo top right).

CHEST LEVER GRIP

Here the edge of the blade points towards the hand's knuckle and the thumb goes firmly onto the flat section of the blade. This grip allows powerful cuts to be made with good control. The hand comes into the chest with the back of the blade facing the chest (the blade facing away), and the cutting motion is away from the body in a controlled style but powerful way, with both arms (see photo, right).

SAFETY FIRST

Always replace your knife in the sheath when not in use.

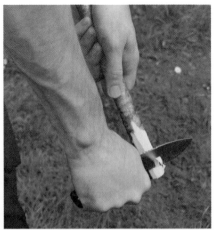
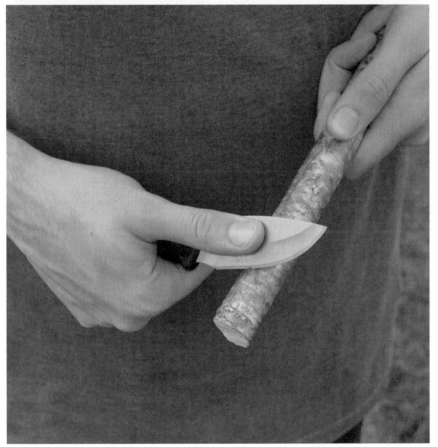

Handy hints...
Knotty terms

Each rope has an end. No surprises there then. The working end is the part used for the knot tying. The opposite end when not in use is the **standing end**. The section between the two ends is the **standing part** while a **bight** is a small curve in the rope. A **loop** is like a bight but crosses over the standing part.

LOOPS AND NOOSES
These are placed around an object or have something connected to them such as a carabiner.

STOPPER KNOTS
Often tied at the end of the line, these handy knots prevent the rope escaping through the opening of a piece of equipment or object.

HITCHES
Used to fasten ropes to other objects, they rely on tension to hold fast.

JAMMING
This is a knot that becomes very difficult to untie after use.

BENDS
These useful knots are the best ones for tying one rope to another.

WHIPPING
A way of protecting the ends of the rope from fraying by binding strong thread around them.

SEIZING
A knot that binds two pieces of rope together side by side, normally to create a loop.

SPLICING
A more permanent way to make loops or join ropes together.

LASHING
The method of securely connecting two or more poles together.

Knots

116
Reef knot

A simple but useful knot to connect two ends of rope of similar size and material. Take the left end over the right and thread under. Then the right end over the left and under again.

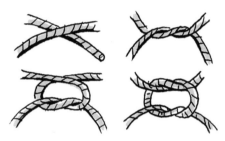

117
Highwayman's hitch

This is a quick-release knot used by horseriders and canoeists. The standing end is connected to the horse, which can pull on the knot but it will not release. Meanwhile, the shorter working end of the rope is for the person to use. A simple tug on this and the whole knot unties itself from the fixed object such as a post. Here's how I was taught this one at Scouts. Create a bight and thread that beneath the post. Put your hand through the bight and grasp the longer (standing) end above the post. Pull this through the bight to create another bight. Put your hand through this second bight and grasp the shorter (working) end. Pull through to create a third bight. Pull tighter with the standing end.

118
Figure of eight

A popular stopper knot that's easy to remember and untie. Hold the top of the rope to create a bight, take the working end around the back of the standing part, bring it back over the top of the standing part, and up through what is now a loop. Pull tight. A rethreaded figure of eight is commonly used by climbers and follows the original shape of the knot. It has a stopper knot at the end.

119
Bowline

A well-used knot that has a non-slip loop at the end, often used in rescue situations. I learned this one at Scouts through the simple saying: "The rabbit comes out of the hole, goes around the tree, and back down the hole." A key part is to get the initial loop correct for the rabbit (the rabbit being the working end of the rope).

120
Clove hitch

A useful way to connect a rope to a post, especially if the load is relatively equal on both ends, and straightforward to tie. One method is to create two identical loops, arrange the second loop beneath the first loop, drop over the post and then tighten both ends.

121
Round turn and two half hitches

This knot is adjustable for length and tightness, and can be used for guy lines. Make a round turn around the object, ideally with the working part

at the bottom. Take the working end over the standing part and through, then repeat further along the standing part so that the working end is sandwiched between the two crossing turns.

122
Fisherman's knot

This knot is used to connect two similar-sized pieces of rope. Lay the ropes side by side, overlapping by several inches. Take the first rope and tie a simple overhand knot in the working end around the other rope.

Repeat the process a few centimetres away, using the second rope to make the overhand knot, ensuring the knot is around the first rope. Pull the other ends of the ropes (the standing ends) together so that the two knots meet in the middle. Pull tight to create the fisherman's knot.

123
Tarbuck

This knot can be used to adjust tension in a tarp or tent guy line. Form a clockwise loop and take the working end of the rope through and around the loop three times.

Bring the working end over the completed turns and around the back of the standing rope, back over itself and effectively through the loop you've just created to tighten.

Handy hints...
Tying knots

PRACTICE MAKES PERFECT
The best way to learn how to tie a knot is to memorise it through practice – over and over again.

KNOW WHAT KNOT TO USE
Becoming skilled with knots brings with it the confidence to use the correct knot in the right situation.

USE DIFFERENT KINDS OF ROPE
Colourful rope of varying lengths and diameters is good to practise on.

TYING POINT
A stick or pole will give you a tying point for your knot work.

PRACTICE UNTYING TOO
This is usually best done by identifying the working end, loosening the knot that's holding it in place and unthreading it. Some knots will be very tough to untie because they are so secure and strong.

124
Knot games

There are a number of fun games that help teach knot skills. You can simply challenge each other to correctly tying a knot behind your back. Alternatively, one of you is blindfolded while the other gives instructions.

125
Edible knots

Carefully practise knot tying using edible laces made from liquorice or long pieces of cooked spaghetti – and you can eat them once knotted.

126
Knots and chocolate

You need a dice and a bar of chocolate. Sit in a circle and take it in turns to throw the dice. When you get a six, start to tie the specified knot, such as a reef knot (page 99). The rest of the group keeps throwing the dice. If the knot is successfully completed before the next six is thrown, the person gets a square of chocolate. If the six is thrown midway through, the rope is passed to that person and the game continues. To add to the fun, the person who gets to eat a chunk of chocolate can only do so by using a knife and fork.

127
Horsing around

One person is the 'horse' while the other is the 'rider'. First, a horizontal pole is set up that your 'horses' will be tied to. Then split into pairs. The rider carries the rope and has a piggyback ride over a distance to the post where they then tie the Highwayman's Hitch knot (page 99). The horse then tests the knot by pulling on the longer (horse) end three times (it should not detach from the post). Once the knot has been successfully tested, the rider remounts and holding the short end, rides off with the rope now disconnected from the post. Quickly swap roles, repeat the challenge and the first pair back wins.

128

Undercover knots

Knots are good to practise in the car on the way to your camping holiday or in the tent if the weather turns bad.

Things to remember...

THE RIGHT ROPE
Always test the strength of the knot and the suitability of the rope.

DOUBLE CHECK
Climbers get their partner to check their knots. If you're depending on the knot for safety, make that a habit.

TAKE GOOD CARE
Look after your rope. Avoid standing on it, ensure it's clean and dry and store it properly in a neat coil.

"Almost every day since you were knee high you've tied knots – doing up your shoe laces, tying up a birthday present for your Mum or Dad or the girl next door. Knots (defined in one dictionary as 'the intertwining of parts of one or more ropes, strings, etc, to fasten them together') are practical things."

The Scout Handbook, 1970

The campfire

129

Make a fire pit

Select a suitable site, taking into account wind direction (accepting wind direction can change) and ideally in a sheltered place but nowhere near other combustible sources.

Clear away anything that could accidentally catch fire and avoid low, overhanging branches. Stones can be used to create the edges of the fire pit and if they are already in place from a previous fire, reuse the spot. Dirt and gravel create a fire bed that can help protect the ground. Remove the turf from the area, roll it up and store it away from sunlight.

130

Build a tipi fire

Place the tinder in first and lay the kindling around it. Push three or four sticks into the ground around it in the shape of a tipi and add more twigs and sticks in the same style, remembering to leave gaps to allow the air (one of the vital ingredients in the 'fire triangle', see page 104), to circulate. Leave a gap at the front – think of it like a door to the tipi – to provide space to ignite the fire. The self-supporting twigs and sticks ensure they do not sit on top of the tinder. Once lit and well underway,

add increasingly larger sticks to the fire in the same tipi pattern while being careful not to smother it.

It's vitally important to properly extinguish the fire. The best way to put it out is to let it burn out completely until it is just ash. Then add water and mix in the dirt, gravel or sand from the fire bed to ensure it is completely extinguished.

If turf has been removed, replace it – you should aim to leave no trace of a fire ever having been lit there.

131

Light it up

Matches or a lighter applied to the tinder is the obvious and easy lighting method, while a fire steel generates a spark to catch in the tinder. Gently blowing on the smoking tinder or initial flames will add further oxygen (part of the fire triangle, see page 104) to help develop the fire. Natural fire-lighting methods such as using a bow and drill take more time and effort.

Handy hints...
Making a fire

THE FIRE TRIANGLE

This is a simple way to remember how fire works. In a nutshell, fire needs three ingredients to burn: fuel, heat and oxygen. Remove any one of those three and the fire will go out.

THE WOOD PILE

Fuel is one of the three vital ingredients of the fire triangle and knowledge of different types of wood is both important and fun to learn. Wood-burning properties vary, but consider factors such as the speed at which it burns and the heat given off, the amount of smoke generated, the scent, brightness and colour of the flame, and quantity of ash produced. Some wood will also burn when green.

Time must be spent collecting the right kind of firewood so that it is to hand when needed, not just at the start but also when the fire is established. Look for dry, dead wood on the ground. Avoid cutting or burning green or wet wood.

Create a log pile and sort the wood into different sizes.

OAK, ASH AND BEECH

Hardwoods provide good, steady heat with glowing embers, which are good for cooking over. Ash is considered the best, and has a low moisture content so will burn from green if necessary. Oak burns slowly, leaving a good bed of hot embers. Stag oak is the seasoned heartwood of trees that have long been dead and can often be found in old forests. However, it's best not to use stag oak since it provides a habitat for bugs and other wildlife.

HAZEL AND SYCAMORE

They give off good heat if thoroughly seasoned and dry.

WILLOW AND ELM

Two to avoid due to the amount of smoke they generate.

LARCH

Scented wood that crackles, and is reasonable for heat.

CONIFER

Has a high resin content so will burn fast and hot but will not leave good embers for cooking. Can also be prone to spitting sparks so keep kit well away if burning evergreen wood.

TINDER

This is the name for the really small stuff that will initially start the fire. It can be composed of wood dust or other materials such as grasses, pine cones or birch bark. Tinder is referred to as 'punk' in the lovely 1953 book *Campcraft for Girl Guides*.

KINDLING

This can consist of primary kindling (matchstick thickness or thinner) and secondary kindling (no more than the thickness of a pencil). These will help establish the fire once the tinder has been lit. It's best to source kindling off the ground, as dead twigs on trees will be drier than those on the ground. Also look out for fallen twigs from trees that have been caught in the branches of another tree. If a twig bends or is hard to snap, it still contains moisture and will be far less effective if at all useful. Use a thumbnail to scrape off some bark – dead wood is brown, green wood is still alive. Collect at least two handfuls of both primary and secondary kindling to ensure your chances of success.

FUEL WOOD

Larger branches or logs that will burn for much longer. 'Dead standing' firewood is offshoots from trunks or branches that are still attached to trees but well rotted, so look out for trees without leaves or buds. You'll know it is dead because it should be easy to remove (with the landowner's permission, of course).

132

Bow and drill method

As with any bushcraft fire-lighting technique, you'll need to improvise with the natural materials to hand.

First create a tinder bundle by working material such as dried grass into the shape of a robin's nest with a hole in the centre.

Take a flat piece of wood such as ivy to create a fireboard. Near the edge of the fireboard, cut a circular depression to house the drill piece. Cut a notch from the depression to the edge of the fireboard to allow the ember (in this case smouldering wood dust) to drop down into an ember pan, such as a piece of birch bark.

Hazel can be used to make the drill and bow. The drill should be stripped of bark and both ends rounded but not sharpened so that it will spin in the depression made in the fireboard. The bow needs strong cord securely tied at either end that is sufficiently slack to twist around the bow for it to then be securely tensioned. A further piece of wood or rock is needed to hold the top of the drill in place when in use. If using wood, cut a small depression in this to help secure the drill.

Improvising with materials to hand will help – a limpet shell, for example, placed between the top piece of

"The camp fire provides the best possible opportunity for introducing good tunes and stories, and for maintaining a fine native tradition in drama, song, and dance."

Campcraft for Girl Guides, 1953

wood and the drill will make it easier to keep the drill firmly in position.

Place the ember pan beneath the notch in the fireboard to catch the smoking tinder, secure the drill into the cord of the bow and place the wood support on top of the bow. If you're right handed, place your right knee on the floor and use your left foot to secure the fireboard. You can hold your left arm around your leg for added stability to help keep the drill firmly in place. Push down hard on the drill and then use a sawing motion with the bow to create friction between the drill and the fireboard.

Effort, concentration and patience are required to keep the saw and drill stable and moving fast to create the smouldering wood dust.

Transfer the contents of the ember pan into the centre of the tinder bundle, close up and gently blow into the bundle to ignite. Place the bundle into the prepared fire pit and gradually build up the flames with the primary and secondary kindling, and then larger pieces of wood.

133
The one-match fire challenge

This is a great test for a group of people. Each group is given just one match to get the fire lit. It's essential to work as a team to carefully collect and prepare the tinder, kindling and fuel wood. Prepare the fire pit, lay the fire and if the chosen team member fails to ignite the fire with one match the group has to undertake a challenge in order to earn a second match. It reinforces the importance of preparation and attention to detail – and when that one and only match is lit, it focuses the mind.

134
Cramp balls

Mother Nature has a way of putting together complementary resources. Ash is the best campfire wood and cramp balls is a fungus that grows almost exclusively on dead ash trees. Although it looks like a small horse dropping it will take a spark from a fire steel, although it must be dry.

135

Cooking trout with bushcraft utensils

If you're cooking on a campfire, think about how you can use the natural materials around you to make utensils. For this dish and cooking method, you'll need a fixed-blade sheath knife and a folding saw plus a fresh trout. Non-toxic wood is required and it's a good reason to become adept at tree identification. Hazel is ideal for utensils, though willow or sycamore are also good.

Using a folding saw (and with the landowner's permission), cut a hazel shoot about a thumb's thickness, taking it from the base of the tree so it will regrow. 'Green' wood also means it will not easily catch fire.

Using a section about 70cm long, sharpen one end ready to embed in the ground. At the other end, use a technique called 'batoning', whereby the knife is placed on the top of the hazel shoot and tapped down using a second stick as a baton (keeping your hands above the blade), gently twisting the knife to separate the two ends. Be careful not to split the wood too far as this section will hold your trout in place.

Use a sheath knife to strip away the bark from the wood to just below the bottom of the split.

Now create the skewers that will keep the fillet open to ensure even cooking. This is done by sharpening small hazel twigs into points and stripping the bark.

To prepare the trout, insert the sheath knife blade into the backside of the fish and cut through the belly towards the head, stopping by the pectoral fin at the gill. Cut around the gill and under the fin up to the top of the head and back down the other side, being careful not to remove the head at this point.

Insert your fingers into the fish from the bottom of the head up towards the top, gently separating the fillet from the spine by pinching and expanding your fingers all the way along the backbone. That way the head and innards of the trout stay in one piece and the fillet detaches neatly with few bones left behind.

The head and innards can go on the fire, leaving you with a neat fillet to insert into your cooking stake.

Place the fillet down the centre of the split branch then skewer it at a right angle to the main stake, each skewer piercing the fish twice, once on either side. Tie some twine around the top of the stake to secure the fish within the split section of the wood.

Push the stake into the ground at an angle (sharpened end first) so the fish cooks above the fire (keep an eye on it in case it falls in). It needs an established fire with hot embers, not directly over the flames. It should take about 15 minutes to cook through and brown nicely. The trout should be beautifully cooked with the added advantage of being lightly smoked.

136

Make your own utensils

You can make tweezer-style utensils called tongs for eating the fish. Use another piece of the hazel, again batoned to split the wood three-quarters of the way down. Strip the bark away from the split section and thin to a point.

Pull out the skewers from the cooked trout, remove the fish from the ground stake and use the tongs to eat it with in a fashion similar to chopsticks but much easier, since they're connected.

137

Try an old poacher's trick

To avoid attracting flies, fish heads and innards should be burned on the fire. However, in a survival situation they can be hung over a pool in a river and will become infested with maggots. The maggots then drop into the river and the trout learn to stick around for a meal before eventually becoming your dinner.

Things to remember...

CHECK THE RULES

When booking a campsite first enquire whether it allows fires or fire pits. Many campsites do not, including Camping and Caravanning Club sites and Camping in the Forest sites. Check with the campsite when you book to avoid disappointment.

KEEP OFF THE GRASS

Fire pits and barbecues often have to be at a specified height to avoid damaging the ground.

SAFETY FIRST

Never leave a fire unattended, and always have a means of dowsing or extinguishing it to hand.

NO SMOKING

Avoid wood that smokes and check the wind direction to be considerate to any neighbours.

TAKE OWNERSHIP

If you are lighting any kind of fire, remind yourself that you alone are responsible for it until it is completely extinguished. That applies to anything from a bonfire to a birthday candle.

Handy hints...
Useful cooking kit

TRIPOD STANDS
These are great to place around a fire. Using adjustable chains, you then hang grills, pots, kettles and billy cans over the fire. Some are also sold with a fire bowl.

FIRE FORKS
Used for grilling sausages, crumpets and similar food over a campfire. They are easily made from wire and you simply insert a suitable stick to make the handle.

RETRO CAMPFIRE KITCHENWARE
Want to glamp up your campfire a little? There are stylish products on the market ideal for campfires, such as enamelled steel pans, kettles and coffee pots complete with matching mugs, bowls and plates.

TRIVETS
To protect the grass from being scorched by hot pans, make yourself a handy trivet. It can be made from three pieces of wood nailed together as a triangle, or four equal-sized sticks used as spars that are tied together with square lashings. Use a clove hitch at the start and end of each lashing (to tie a clove hitch see page 100). Alternatively, invest in a metal trivet that can be kept on the edge of the campfire where you can rest your frying pan or pots.

FIRELIGHTERS
Easy to forget, whichever way you choose to light the campfire. Matches and a lighter are a must if you don't plan to start the fire by an alternative, more natural, method.

BUCKET OF WATER
To help with burns and to use if the fire gets a bit out of control.

Storytelling around the campfire

138
Get creative

Campfires make the ideal backdrop for creating an exciting, magical atmosphere. The sights, sounds and smells of the flames and the night air are perfect accompaniments to stories, so make sure you use them for maximum effect.

139
Whisper key sections

Use your voice softly at first to create intrigue and then get louder. Occasional unexpected shrieks at the right moment will ensure the audience keeps on their toes.

140
Be animated

Use exaggerated facial expressions and gesticulate with your hands and arms. Get up and walk around the circle, stopping at key moments for maximum dramatic effect.

141
Draw on your surroundings

Take additional inspiration from the dark night sky, unusual sounds from nocturnal wildlife, the crackle of the burning wood, twinkling stars, the shape of the moon, and dancing shadows cast by the fire. They are all there to stoke the story.

142
Use sound effects

Ring a little bell or hit tent pegs together for a clang. Snap a twig or scrunch some leaves. Scrape a stick along the ground.

143
Make eye contact

Don't be afraid to stare deeply into the eyes of every member of your audience in turn.

144
Take along a prop

This could be an old family photograph or an unusual artifact. Centre the story on it, or get one of the kids to invent a story for it first and then tell your own pre-prepared tale.

Handy hints...
Telling tales

KEY INGREDIENTS
When dreaming up stories consider the key ingredients for a good tale:

CHOOSE A NARRATOR
Who is telling your story? Will you be yourself or will you adopt a character to tell it on your behalf?

HAVE A STRONG OPENING
You don't want to lose your audience at the first hurdle.

THINK ABOUT THE CHARACTERS
Make them identifiable and likeable (or not). And keep the number of characters to a level where all can remember them.

WHAT IS THE PLOT?
There needs to be drama, intrigue, tension and then a release from that apprehension. Events tend to get worse before they get better. A simple sub-plot can add an extra dimension to the tale.

WHERE IS THE STORY SET?
If you think about the historical period as well as the location you could get really descriptive if you read up on it beforehand.

CONSIDER THE ROLE PLAYED BY HUMOUR
Is there a place for it in your story? Should the whole yarn be funny?

THINK ABOUT THE ENDING
All stories need an ending, so make sure you have a good finale in mind from the start. A campfire tale is typically short so in a small space of time the narrator will need to cover a range of emotions – highs and lows. Keep the pace going, get the audience on the edge of their collective seat and then reveal the ending.

GIVE THE STORY A TWIST
Finish it in an unexpected way. Turn the story on its head with the hero becoming the villain or the narrator suddenly becoming untrustworthy. Open endings can be good as they prompt questions from inquisitive young minds. Ask them what *they* think happened next.

"After the meal, the whole party, on a quiet summer's evening, will sit round, and songs without a sting, and stories without obscenity, will be rendered and told."

Thomas Hiram Holding
Author of *The Campers' Handbook*, published in 1908, and founder of The Camping and Caravanning Club

145

Add a touch of torchlight

A beam of light can illuminate 'something' in the trees for added suspense and intrigue: "Did you see that?" Meanwhile, the use of a red beam will create a different ambience. Introduce light and sound when the audience is least expecting it for dramatic effect.

146

Get everyone involved

Storytelling is something that can be done aged four or 94. Ask the family to have a think about their tale during the day, telling them that they each have five minutes to tell it that evening.

147

Audience participation

Tip off fellow grown-ups to give hisses, boos and cheers in the correct places to encourage the kids to do the same.

148

Story-making circles

Start with one person and go around the campfire getting each person in turn to add just one sentence.

Set simple rules, such as how many rounds there will be and how many characters are allowed. Challenge everyone to introduce one character and make sure the last person knows they need to add a twist to the tale.

149

FFF (family fantasy fable)

Write exciting words on pieces of paper – for example 'giant', 'shipwreck' or 'exploded'. Fold them up and put them into a pot. Each member of the family picks one out and has to create a short story around the word. Alternatively, one person picks out a word to start the story and after two minutes, the next person picks out a new word to continue the tale. Repeat this process until everyone has had a turn and the last person creates the ending. You've created your own family fantasy fable.

Things to remember...

STAY WARM AND DRY
It's the only way to keep the audience's attention. Consider putting another adult on hot drinks duty too.

PITCH IT RIGHT
Know your audience. Don't scare the children – they will struggle to sleep.

Singing around the campfire

150

Rounds

Singing rounds is a fun and hopefully harmonious way to sing a song.

Practise first with a simple tune such as *Row, Row, Row Your Boat*, each new singer joining in with the first line when the previous person completes their first line:

Row, row, row your boat
Gently down the stream
Merrily, merrily, merrily, merrily
Life is but a dream.

It's a simple tune but you can play around with it to add interest. For example, once the last person has finished, everyone repeats the last line, making it fade in volume.

Try also *London's Burning*:

London's burning, London's burning
Fetch the engines, fetch the engines
Fire fire, fire fire
Pour on water, pour on water.

151

Folk songs

Keep alive traditional music such as this Scottish folk song, great for an easy-to-learn option.

MY BONNIE LIES OVER THE OCEAN
My Bonnie lies over the ocean
My Bonnie lies over the sea
My Bonnie lies over the ocean
Oh bring back my Bonnie to me.

Chorus:
Bring back, bring back
Bring back my Bonnie to me, to me
Bring back, bring back
Bring back my Bonnie to me.

Last night as I lay on my pillow
Last night as I lay on my bed
Last night as I lay on my pillow
I dreamt that my Bonnie was dead.

(Repeat chorus)

Oh blow the winds o'er the ocean
And blow the winds o'er the sea
Oh blow the winds o'er the ocean
And bring back my Bonnie to me.

(Repeat chorus)

The winds have blown over the ocean
The winds have blown over the sea
The winds have blown
over the ocean
And brought back
my Bonnie to me.

152

The Fox

Believed to be from an old English poem that dates back to the 15th century:

The fox went out on a chilly night,
He prayed for the moon to give him light,
For he'd many a mile to go that night,
Before he reached the town-o, town-o, town-o,
He'd many a mile to go that night,
Before he reached the town-o.

He ran 'til he came to a great big pen,
Where the ducks and the geese were put therein,
"A couple of you will grease my chin,
Before I leave this town-o, town-o, town-o,
A couple of you will grease my chin,
Before I leave this town-o."

He grabbed the grey goose by the neck,
Throwed a duck across his back,
He didn't mind their quack, quack, quack,
And their legs a-dangling down-o, down-o, down-o,
He didn't mind their quack, quack, quack,
And their legs a-dangling down-o.

Then old Mother Flipper-Flopper jumped out of bed,
Out of the window she cocked her head,
Crying, "John, John! The grey goose is gone,
And the fox is on the town-o, town-o, town-o!"
Crying, "John, John! The grey goose is gone,
And the fox is on the town-o!"

Then John, he went to the top of the hill,
Blowed his horn both loud and shrill,
The fox he said, "I better flee with my kill,
Or they'll soon be on my trail-o, trail-o, trail-o!"
The fox he said, "I better flee with my kill,
Or they'll soon be on my trail-o!"

He ran 'til he came to his cosy den,
There were the little ones, eight, nine, ten,
They said, "Daddy, better go back again,
'Cause it must be a mighty fine town-o, town-o, town-o!"
They said, "Daddy, better go back again,
'Cause it must be a mighty fine town-o!"

Then the fox and his wife without any strife,
Cut up the goose with a fork and knife,
They never had such a supper in their life,
And the little ones chewed on the bones-o, bones-o, bones-o,
They never had such a supper in their life,
And the little ones chewed on the bones-o.

153
Nature's orchestra

Add a fun element of musical accompaniment with nature's own percussion orchestra. Gather some acorns or conkers and add them to a plastic tub with a lid for a shaker. Different materials will give your orchestra different sounds.

Introduce your own wind section by stretching a long blade of grass between the top and bottom of both thumbs, cupping your hands together and blowing across the blade of grass to create a high-pitched sound. Or use different-sized pieces of fallen wood to create a mini glockenspiel, complete with sticks for mallets.

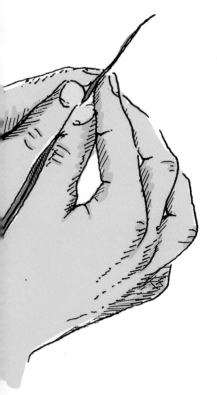

154
Folk who like folk

The Camping and Caravanning Club has a special interest section called the Folk Dance and Song Group. It's aimed at people who want to combine folk music and dance, plus art and crafts, with camping. The group's members are happy to share their knowledge and skills – it's a great way to pass traditional skills and songs down to future generations.

155
Classic alternatives

Throw in a few more up-to-date songs to bridge the generation gap:
- *American Pie*, Don McLean (a folk-rock classic)
- *Don't Stop Me Now*, Queen (fun to join in with the chorus)
- *Happy*, Pharrell Williams
- *Hometown Glory*, Adele (a beautiful, stirring song)
- *Better Together*, Jack Johnson (lovely accompanied by a guitar)

156
And finally...

Learn to play the harmonica for a true 'outdoorsy' sound that's ideal for a campfire singalong. Or go camping with someone who can play one.

4
GAMES &
ACTIVITIES

> ## "Through these games, apart from their health- and joy-giving properties, we can instil the sense of fair play, discipline and self-control – in a word good sportsmanship, among our future men."
>
> Sir Robert Baden-Powell
> Founder of the Scouts and President of The Camping and Caravanning Club 1919-1940,
> *Scouting Games*, sixth edition

The best sound a parent can hear – ever – is the sound of their own children laughing. It cannot be beaten. Nothing even comes close. And happy children means happy parents (not forgetting grandparents too).

Camping is a fantastic way for kids to get happy. The Camping and Caravanning Club's Real Richness report found that more than 90 per cent of those surveyed said that camping represented fun for the entire family. So camping is brilliant for having fun, reconnecting with nature, getting active outdoors and making new friends. And there's one simple activity that combines all those things at once – play. It doesn't have to be the boisterous, noisy and active kind of play. Instead, it can embrace make-believe, storytelling, crafts, cards or board games, any of which will come into their own if the weather is bad and you are likely to be cooped up in the tent for a while.

Board not bored

For the parents of the computer-game generation there is good news. Despite the proportion of kids spending time playing electronic games on screens doubling in a generation, a survey in 2015 found that two out of three would still like to learn how to play traditional board games.

Even though most campsites provide easy access to electric hook-ups and therefore the ability to recharge a computer-game device, there's no doubting that camping holidays can help break children free from such devices, even if only temporarily. There's the countryside to explore, new friends to make on a campsite, camping skills to learn, activities to pursue, attractions to visit – and then there's the humble board game.

Children want their parents' undivided attention. And that's where a board game delivers – it brings all the family together around the camping table for quality time together and a healthy dose of competition.

So it's time to ditch the tech, especially if the weather's bad, and dig out the traditional games involving boards, dice and a humble pack of cards that will take up next to no space in your camping luggage and yet provide a really surprising assortment of fun, challenges and tricks. They are an ideal partner for camping trips and top wet-weather companions.

Pack a pack (or two)

My grandparents taught me a number of card games that I loved playing as a youngster. And how many of us as children tried to copy the impressively fast shuffling skills of grown-ups? Unfortunately the passage of time means that we forget most of the games we played in childhood and their rules, which makes card games another subject to share and pass down to our own families. And as with any card game, there are variations to the rules, including to the games here, so be sure to agree them before you start.

Some games are based on pure chance while others need strategy or quick reflexes in order to win. Just be wary of any teenager asking to play 52 Card Pick-Up. That's a game no-one forgets in a hurry.

Historic days out

History is a great subject for enquiring young minds. And there's no better way to discover it than by bringing it to life – seeing it, touching it, smelling it and even tasting it for yourself. And it's easy to do.

There are many campsites in the grounds of castles and stately homes, and even more just a short walk or drive away, making a camping holiday an ideal time to learn more about what shaped the nation. Themed events, battle re-enactments and special family open days that bring history to life are staged year-round the length and breadth of the country. So if you want a day out packed with myths and legends to really get the imagination going, just head to a historic site for your own form of time travel.

There are a number of excellent campsites located close to some of Britain's most impressive castles, such as Culzean Castle in Ayrshire; Corfe in Dorset; Llanystumdwy in Gwynedd; Scone in Tayside; Jedburgh in the Scottish Borders; Barnard Castle in Country Durham; and Salisbury in Wiltshire.

Stone circles and ancient burial sites

These can often be found deep in the countryside, tucked right out of the way. A very vivid imagination is required to envisage the time of their creation thousands of years ago. It's thought that stone circles were built for ceremonial reasons, and some will align with the points of the compass or sun movements. How were they built? What was life like at the time? Why are they spiritual places? These, and many more, are great questions for young history detectives to investigate on a day away from the campsite. Use those questions to dream up answers that form the basis of a storytelling session.

Trenches and war cemeteries

If you are camping abroad, France and Belgium in particular offer many locations for visiting preserved World War I trench systems and war cemeteries. There are also plenty of historic sites and cemeteries to visit for World War II. It's important to learn the lessons of history and these places really bring home the harsh realities of war to young people.

Why not use your own family history to highlight much more personal connections? I've camped in northern France and explored battle sites with my two sons and

friends following an old map, itinerary and photo album that my great-grandfather had kept from an old comrades' reunion tour. We had a range of photographs of him together with his campaign medals, which are all pictured above, and they provided a rich source of clues to help us build a picture of his travels during and after the war. The back of one of his campaign medals even provided essential information that enabled us to track down his war records at the National Archive at Kew.

During that camping trip we were able to retrace some of his steps during active service and also later in the 1950s on battlefield tours with his old comrades. Whenever we stopped at war cemeteries, we tasked the boys with locating the specific graves of servicemen such the youngest soldier (there was a 14-year-old boy buried at one cemetery we visited), and the grave of a captain who was twice awarded the Victoria Cross – one of only three men to twice win Britain's highest award for bravery.

We've also visited trenches off the beaten track in Slovenia's Triglav National Park during a motorhome tour and tried to imagine life as a soldier in World War I surrounded by such stunning mountainous scenery.

Wet weather fun

If there are days when everything is damp outside, perhaps even drenched, it doesn't have to mean that family fun comes to an abrupt halt. There's plenty of enjoyment still to be had inside your tent or caravan awning. Don't be tempted to reach for the tech when the showers start. Instead, think about playing some good old-fashioned games.

The key is to do some homework in advance and sketch out a loose timetable of wet-weather activities. Come up with a plan for each day and get the kids involved – that way they'll see that even if the weather is bad they're still going to have a great time.

Prepare a Plan B

Advance planning will also help Mum and Dad. If there's a Plan B in place they will feel more confident and relaxed for those occasions when the weather simply won't play ball. A Plan B has another important element: be prepared to scrap the plan completely if the sun suddenly starts shining and all everyone wants to do is just hit the beach.

Nature's palette

If bad weather is forecast but you can still get out and about, make time to look carefully at the plant life around the campsite and you'll find nature's palette there just waiting to be used for colourful creations. Paintings, drawings, collages – they're all great activities to enjoy and there is a surprising amount of natural material to hand that is fun to use for art and crafts, as well as costing nothing.

Artwork is an ideal wet-weather activity that can easily be enjoyed inside the tent or caravan. Ideally pick a dry day to go gathering – collect sticks, leaves, acorns, pebbles, feathers, flowers, pieces of bark (the list is endless) – and get crafting, especially when it rains. It's not only fun but also it brings children closer to nature. Working with nature's palette means they'll learn more about the plant life while also creating lovely keepsakes of the camping holiday.

Budding young snappers

. . . .

"To be plain, camping as a pastime, like photography, must be done carefully and well, or it is best not touched."

Thomas Hiram Holding
Author of *The Campers' Handbook*, published in 1908,
and founder of The Camping and Caravanning Club

. . . .

How times have changed. When Thomas Hiram Holding wrote those words more than a century ago, the Eastman Kodak Company had not long introduced the first iconic box-shaped Brownie camera. It cost just $1 (film was 15 cents a roll) and with it came the birth of photography as an affordable pastime that pretty much everyone could enjoy.

Our fascination with photography has changed little since but the technology certainly has. Today, high-resolution cameras are commonplace on smartphones, and pictures can be shared with the world in a matter of seconds. The use of them in drones has changed the way we look at our landscapes while action cams mean we can capture the excitement of our exploits on outdoor adventures with a lightweight device strapped to our heads. Or the dog for that matter.

As for Holding's comment about camping as a pastime, well, it's never been more varied, accessible and popular. Cameras are perfect for capturing those outdoor moments to create a lasting reminder of great times and to share with friends and family. Photography slows us down so that we notice the detail in life – the colours and shades, sunlight, movement, texture...

By taking pictures of wildlife and the countryside children become more aware of their natural surroundings, which in turn helps that rewilding process. If you've just taken a great picture of a magpie moth, you're much more likely to remember its name, though the same might not be true of its Latin name (*Abraxas grossulariata* by the way).

So spend a day focusing on the fun things and let the kids get behind the camera lens. And that's the key – make it fun. It doesn't matter what type of camera you have or how good it is, just get snapping.

Candid camera

The beauty of digital cameras is that you are no longer restricted to the limitations and the cost of rolls of film. So you can merrily snap away. This particularly comes in handy when photographing people naturally without them looking at the camera.

Candid photography is fun but quite a skill as you need to blend into the background. It's always courteous to let people know you're taking their picture first, and at the same time ask them to forget about you being there, in the nicest possible way. I find that if you have a digital camera set to sport mode, you can click away at a subject with the hope that one of many pictures will work. Zoom lenses also help. Use something in the foreground to frame your picture, such as a dry-stone wall or branch to add depth, frame an edge of the photo and make it look more natural.

When downloading and sorting out your digital pictures, remember that there's plenty of software available to edit the image. So if you have taken a great natural photo of someone but the rest of the image is untidy, crop in close to the strong section and save that as your photo.

Campfire gatherings, the camping dinner table, play time, pitching the tent – all are ideal situations in which to take candid photos of friends and family because people are interacting and doing things within the context of your holiday. Get the right shot – a gappy smile of a young cousin who's just lost their two front teeth or granddad getting melted marshmallow from a s'more down his chin – and it will be worthy of the photo frame back home.

Show and tell

These days, processing a roll of film and expectantly awaiting the results (good and bad) is a distant memory. Now, you have the camera's memory card to contend with and it's crammed with colourful photographs thanks to the kids getting snap happy to record their camping adventures. At this point it's all too easy to download them onto a computer, file – and forget.

Don't let that happen. Instead bring those photographs to life by encouraging your children to transform their creations into lasting mementos. Putting together a campsite photo album can tell a story about the whole camping adventure or a single day out.

The pictures will also be great for 'show and tell' at school the following week or for staging a family slideshow to bring back happy memories for all. It can be tough to get away from tech these days and so embrace it – take along a laptop to help sort and edit the photos in the evening or during a rainy day.

And if you want to take a fun photographic challenge to another level, why not make a film? A holiday video is a fantastic way to encourage children to tell their own stories through moving pictures.

Outdoor games

157

The Matchbox Challenge

How many items from around the campsite can be fitted into an empty matchbox? Naturally a number of empty matchboxes will be required together with some imagination. Then challenge the kids to set off around the campsite in search of tiny items to jam inside. Is the pebble too big for the matchbox to shut? Can a piece of string be cut down to make more space for other items? Set a time to be back at the tent and award a prize for the most items. Have a bonus prize too for the most unusual object.

158

Cracking fun

In the weeks before the holiday, collect a number of empty cardboard egg boxes and paint each 'dimple' (the part in which the eggs sit) a different colour. Each box could have a blue, yellow, red, green, brown and white section, for example. At the campsite, give each of the young children an egg box and challenge them to collect as many different things as they can find that both fit into the dimple and correspond with the colours.

159

Deer stalking

This is an old Scout game that's best played in a small wood or copse. One person is the deer and heads off into the wood to await detection but without hiding or crouching down, though they can occasionally move short distances. The other players need to approach from different directions, ideally using the vegetation as cover, to track down and then gradually stalk the deer. Using sight and sound, the deer looks out for the stalkers and when one is spotted, he or she shouts out and points to their position. If correct that stalker stands up and the game continues until either all stalkers have been identified or someone has got close enough to tag the deer.

A time limit can be set and once that's reached, all the stalkers need to reveal themselves and identify their positions. The closest to the deer wins. The less time available, the faster the game is played.

A variation is to blindfold the deer and play the game on ground that has lots of dry twigs and stones. The deer uses hearing to point in the direction of the stalker. If correct, the stalker is out of the game. The remaining players continue until the time is up, in which case they see who is the closest, or the deer is tagged. This is the type of game that's also good for a grown-up to umpire (unless of course they want to join in).

160

A family quest

Set aside at least half a day to stage a family quest. Whatever the age of your children, there are plenty of ideas within these pages to help you create your own quest, which could be imaginative and even fantastical. Here's one I dreamed up.

We pitch up at a campsite in Staffordshire on the edge of Cannock Chase, England's smallest Area of Outstanding Natural Beauty, that's run by the Forestry Commission.

The dawn chorus wakes us so we make an early start, tiptoeing quietly off the campsite for a picnic breakfast that was prepared the night before.

We give the quest a name – Our Chase Through Cannock – and follow a map for a themed woodland walk (the kind you pick up at tourist centres for specified trails or can download from the internet and print off at home). I will have already written challenges on the map at specified points along the way.

The children are in charge of the navigation and, at waymarked points, have to use a branch to tie three knots (pages 98-100), identify the song of a bird (page 59) and build a simple den (page 88). We will also capture our quest on camera in the form of a 'vlog' (page 156).

After a picnic lunch our route will bring us back close to the campsite, where we follow a series of clues and cyphers to find some treasure –

otherwise known as sweets – hidden back at the tent before we set off.

Create your family quest in advance at home with a downloaded trail map. Also download the Forestry Commission's free ForestXplorer app to add some digital fun to your quest. If you have a budding tree detective in the family, try out the app's tree identifier function too.

Things to remember...

CAMPSITE ETIQUETTE

Most campsites have playing fields or designated play areas to ensure ball games and other noisier fun activities are kept away from pitches (that's pitches of the camping variety rather than football type). This is to avoid potential damage and to keep things quiet and peaceful for other campers.

161

Cricketing capers

Cricket is a great team game ideal for families but it needs stumps or at least some sort of wicket. So if you don't have those, try French cricket instead – it's fun and fast-paced and the wicket is your legs. You still need a bat or tennis racket and a soft ball such as a tennis ball.

The aim is to score as many 'runs' as possible before being bowled or caught out.

The batsman stands in the middle and the other players surround him or her as fielders. A person bowls with the aim of hitting the person's legs with the ball below the knee. When the batsman strikes the ball, he or she accumulates runs by passing the bat around their body, switching hands behind their back. Each time it counts as one run.

As soon as the ball is back with a fielder in position, that person then bowls.

A batsman can only rotate his or her position when the ball is not in anyone's hand. So if they are facing the wrong direction, the ball can still be bowled and the batsman must try to defend their legs (and score some runs if they're lucky). The batting duties change hands when either the legs are hit or the ball is caught.

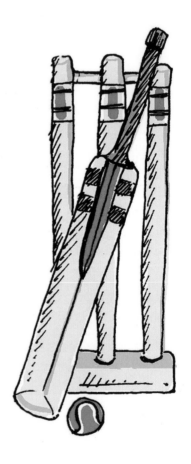

Things to remember...

There are a few items that you really mustn't forget to pack if you want to play a variety of outdoor games on your camping holiday...

A BAT AND BALL

Absolutely essential for rounders, cricket and its French counterpart (see left).

QUOITS

If you are looking for some simple but competitive family fun, the game of quoits is suitable for the very young and the very old. It's even better if they play together.

CROQUET

For something a bit posher on sultry summer days and evenings.

PEN AND PAPER

So that an impartial observer can keep a running score.

PRIZES

For the winners and runners-up. Remember to reward effort, too, and even consider awarding a booby prize for the person who came last in the most games!

Handy hints...
Invent your own games

Making up your own games can be a fun activity in its own right. Here's what to think about:

COME UP WITH THE CONCEPT

How do you win? How long should it take to get to that point?

DEVISE THE RULES

How many players are involved and what are they allowed to do (and just as importantly, what are they definitely not allowed to do)?

INVENT A NAME

Call it something wacky and exciting.

WHAT WILL IT NEED?

Can you make any necessary equipment yourself?

TRY IT OUT

Test it on your friends and family, and fine-tune the concept and rules. Let any new campsite friends know where and when you'll be playing it. Then enjoy the fun.

Board games

162
Snakes & Ladders

This worldwide classic derives from an ancient Indian board game. Players aim to move from the starting square at the bottom of the board to the finishing square at the top, helped or hindered by climbing up ladders and sliding down slippery snakes, which could take them 'back to square one'.

Family friction factor: Medium to high. The constant snake-shaped setbacks frustrate some younger children.

Handy hints...
For playing Snakes & Ladders

IT'S JUST A GAME!
There's no real skill involved, only luck, so teach kids to keep their cool when the snakes come thick and fast.

163
Monopoly

Created in the US in 1902, Monopoly was originally known as The Landlord's Game, based on buying, selling and developing land. Today's Monopoly is made by Hasbro and there are a number of modern variations, though I like the older classic sets, and a junior set will get younger ones off to a good start.

Family friction factor: High! Extremely competitive, it offers a fascinating insight into your children's personalities and their receptiveness to risk-taking.

Handy hints...
For playing Monopoly

MATHS SKILLS
Encourage one of the kids to be the banker to help maths skills.

SEAL THE DEAL
Give kids pointers on negotiation skills and securing a good deal.

GO LOCAL
Use sticky notes to rewrite the place names with local names.

164

Scrabble

Scrabble was trademarked in the US as a game in 1948 and quickly grew in popularity. Up to four people can play by taking it in turns to form words using tiles in rows from left to right or downward columns, connected to existing words. Points are earned according to the allotted value of letters. It's great for learning new words and spellings, and also for simple maths skills.

Family friction factor: Medium. It's competitive like Monopoly but there are usually fewer reasons to spark off an argument.

Handy hints...
For playing Scrabble

DOWNLOAD A DICTIONARY
Disagreements tend to centre on whether or not a word appears in the dictionary. Since you're unlikely to remember to pack a dictionary, download an app version instead before you set off.

AIM HIGH
Focus on high-scoring squares on the board to maximise the score.

EXTEND YOURSELF
Remember word extensions. Camp can become Campfire while Motor can extend to Motorhome.

RIGHT ON Q
The letter Q is worth 10 points – swot up on words that include it.

165

The Battleship game

A popular naval strategy game that dates back to World War I and was first played on paper. Decades later plastic games were introduced, followed by electronic and then online versions. A player randomly pinpoints and then sinks their opponent's vessels. It gets especially exciting when both players are closing in with hits on each other's final ship.

Family friction factor: Low. Only two people can play it and they tend to be too deep in thought to argue as they as seek out their opponent's navy.

Handy hints...
For playing the Battleship game

MAKE SOME SPACE

Space out your own ships and face them in different directions to minimise the chances of a hit.

CONFUSE YOUR OPPONENT

Alternatively, confuse your opponent by placing them side by side but in different directions.

BUILD UP THE HITS

Once you've scored a hit on your opponent, work subsequent shots around the immediate area of the strike until you've sunk the ship.

166

Make your own Battleship game while on holiday

Why not go retro and create your own paper version? You'll need four pieces of squared paper (two each). The pages each need identical grids of 12 squares, one axis marked A-L, the other 1 to 12. If you use the pages from an old maths textbook, you won't need to draw out the grids.

Each player has an ocean upon which to mark their own battleships: five squares for an aircraft carrier, four for a battleship, three for both a submarine and destroyer, and two for a minesweeper. Ensure your opponent cannot see this sheet as it's what they will be aiming at.

Take it in turns to fire, for example, calling "B4". You mark your own shots on your second piece of paper. If it's a hit, your opponent must declare it, so mark it differently to a miss (ticks and crosses or different colour pens work best). You should continue firing in that area until the vessel is sunk. Again, your opponent must tell you when that has happened.

The ocean sheet with your own battleships must also be marked to track your opponent's shots. The winner is the first person to sink the entire fleet.

167

Shut the Box

A simple dice-based game involving a counting box, tactics and a healthy dose of mental arithmetic. Players use the combined total of the dice throw to close down numbers in the box. For example, a total dice throw of seven could close a 1, 2 and 4.

Family friction factor: Medium. It's exciting and can get quite vocal.

Handy hints...
For playing
Shut the Box

BEFORE YOU START

Set a number of rounds to play.

WINNERS AND LOSERS

The overall winner gets a treat while the loser is set a fun forfeit.

168

Pass the Pigs

This involves rolling two model porkers in the same way as dice to achieve a score. It's simple, uncomplicated fun and definitely not a boar!

169

Cluedo

Devised in the 1940s in England, it's a classic murder mystery whodunnit. Characters include Miss Scarlet and Colonel Mustard and the weapons range from a candlestick to a revolver, while the rooms in the mansion include the billiard room, ballroom and library. Players have to move around the board (the mansion) gathering clues. They ultimately deduce the outcome in a race against each other. Who was the killer, what weapon did they use and in which room was the fiendish crime committed? Play the detective to find out.

Family friction factor: Low. Everyone is concentrating too hard on unravelling the mystery to worry much about arguing.

Handy hints...
For playing Cluedo

PAIR UP

Pair up as parent and child to help explain the rules and concepts.

GET A ROOM

You can only play detective once you're in a room, so if you've sniffed out the murderer, that's where to spend time.

USE THE SECRET PASSAGES

These guarantee you moving straight to another room.

PIECE IT TOGETHER

Pay close attention to other players' suggestions. The more precise notes you make, the more aspects of the crime you can piece together.

HAVE A POKER FACE

If you hit upon the answer to a clue, don't make it look too obvious to your opponents when you write it down. Calmly make a note.

170

Dominoes

Great for maths skills when playing 'threes and fives' and using a pegging board to keep the score. And when you're fed up, stand them up on their ends and, with a steady hand, create lines for some domino toppling.

171

Invest in a compendium

This will bring you hours of variety and entertainment in one box!

Things to remember...

WHICH WAY UP?

Decide the best way the board should face (not everyone can read upside down, especially youngsters).

SLOW IT DOWN

If you have over-enthusiastic dice rollers remain calm. Put a blanket or cloth on the table to slow it down a little, though you'll need to brace yourself for the disagreements about rolled dice that are not sitting flat. Use an egg cup or tumbler for shaking your dice.

AGREE THE RULES

Agree any rules (and variations) in advance of the game.

TURN A BLIND EYE

Don't cheat (parents) but expect to turn a blind eye to children 'bending' the rules.

BE PREPARED TO BACK DOWN

Mum and Dad, be prepared to back down. Competitive parents have their place but keep on the right side of that fine line. And remember, nobody likes a gloater!

Card games

172

Fancy shuffling

Handling a pack of cards with confidence helps younger children to improve their dexterity. Shuffling and dealing also makes them feel in control of the game.

This impressive way to shuffle a pack takes practiCe, which is all part of the fun.

Split the pack into two roughly equal halves.

Grip your thumbs at the top ends, facing each other while the middle and ring fingers hold the bottom ends. Meanwhile use your index fingers to push down in the centre of the cards.

Place the two corners close together and strum your thumbs up across the edges of the cards on both sides. If you start one side fractionally before the other, the corners of the cards should interlay.

Blend them together just at the top so the entire thumb ends are interlaid to make one long pack of cards.

Neaten the edges and ensure each end is in the palm of your hands with thumbs on top. Push the fingers of both hands upwards on the middle interlaid section of cards holding the ends firmly with your palms.

Release your fingers to allow the cards to quickly flick down with a rasping sound. Lastly, neaten up the pack.

Repeat several times for ultimate dramatic effect.

173

Newmarket

A classic game, often noisy, for three players and upwards.

Overall winner: The person at the end of a specified number of rounds with the most counters.

You'll need a bag of counters, coins or even acorns or conkers collected on a woodland walk, and each player first receives an equal amount.

Two packs of cards are required. The first pack is your main set while you'll also need the Ace, King, Queen and Jack, all different suits, from the second pack. These four cards – the 'horses' – are placed face up in the centre of the table and each player adds a counter (or more) to their chosen horse card before the round begins. Aces are high.

The dealer then dishes out all the cards even if the amount varies for players, and includes a dummy hand.

The person to the left of the dealer starts by placing their lowest card down in front of them, face up, and calls it out. For example, "the four of hearts". The player with the five of hearts then places the card down in front of them (all players keep separate piles). This continues until either the Ace of that suit is played or no-one has the next card because it's in the dummy hand.

When this happens the person who laid the last card starts a new suit

with their lowest card (if they cannot go because they don't have a new suit the play continues with the person to their left).

The winner of the round is the person who has no cards left. Each of their opponents must then give the winner a counter for each card they have left over.

When someone plays a 'horse' card they collect all its counters (or acorns). If at the end of the game there are counters left on horse cards, they remain in play.

Players begin a new round by adding more counters to their chosen horse so the counters begin to accumulate, and a new hand is dealt.

After a specified number of rounds, the counters are added up to reveal the overall winner.

174

Beggar thy Neighbour

A game of chance for two.

The winner: The player who holds all the cards.

Deal the pack. Each player holds their hand face down and takes it in turns to turn a card from the top and lay it face up in a central stack. When a penalty card is laid (an Ace, King, Queen or Jack) the other player must 'pay' by adding more cards to the stack: four for an Ace, three for Kings, two for Queens, one for Jacks.

The person who played the penalty card picks up the stack and adds them to the bottom of their hand. However, if another penalty card is played while paying out, the other person pays the penalty. Whoever runs out of cards first loses.

175

Crazy Eights

An easy game for two or more players.

The winner: The player who is the first to play all their cards.

The dealer dishes out five cards each, face down, or seven if only two people are playing. The remaining cards are placed in the middle, face down, and the top card turned over and laid beside the pile. If that card is an eight, it gets buried in the middle of the stack and the next card is turned over.

If the first card turned over is the 10 of Clubs, for example, the first player (to the left of the dealer) has to play either a Club or a 10. If another 10 is played the game continues but in that same suit.

If a person is unable to play, they take a card from the central pile and continue

to do so until they can make a move. They lay that card and play continues.

All eights are wild cards and can be played at any point. When it's laid the player must specify a suit.

If the central pile runs out, the last card is taken off the top and placed face up to continue the game, and the remainder shuffled and placed face down on the table.

The winner is the first person to lay their last card.

176

Old Maid

Kids will love trying to avoid being the Old Maid. For two or more players.

The winner: Anyone who discards all his or her cards is safe. The loser is the one left with the Old Maid card.

Using a standard pack, remove one of the Queens. That leaves two of the same colour, and the one remaining single-colour Queen – the Old Maid.

Deal all the cards, even if some have more than others. Everyone sorts out their cards into pairs of equal rank, such as a pair of Jacks, and lays them down. If a player has all four cards of the same rank, for example all the fives, they lay them down as two pairs. If three cards are held, they lay one pair and hang on to the third card.

The dealer goes first and turns to the player on their left and, without showing the cards, fans them out. The facing player randomly selects one of the cards. If they can then make a pair from that card, they lay it down. If they cannot, they keep it. That player then turns to the next person on their left and the game continues.

The aim is to lay down all your cards in pairs until you have none left. When that happens you're safe and you drop out of the game.

Fellow players continue until they too drop out. Ultimately, all the cards will be paired with one exception – the Old Maid. Whoever is left with this card loses and is crowned the Old Maid.

177

Learn a few card tricks

Holidays mean time on your hands to practise a trick or two. Encourage kids to learn some from a book or the internet, and then perform them in a magic show for friends and family.

178

Snap: The simplest of the lot

Snap is a loud, active game that's great even for little ones and is best played at speed. There are various ways to play but this is how I was taught.

The winner: The player who has all the cards in their hand.

Shuffle the pack and deal all the cards face down to the players. They mustn't look at them. The person to the left of the dealer goes first by turning over their top card and placing it in the centre. The next player then turns their card and, without looking at it too soon, places it on the centre pile. If it's not a matching card, the game continues in turn. When there is a matching card you shout 'snap!' and quickly place your hand on the central stack. You can include a rule to penalise anyone who mistakenly shouts 'snap!' by making them give one of their cards to each other player.

The first person to successfully shout 'snap!' wins the cards in the middle and places them on the bottom of their own hand. When a player runs out of cards they leave the game though the round continues. The winner must hold all the cards.

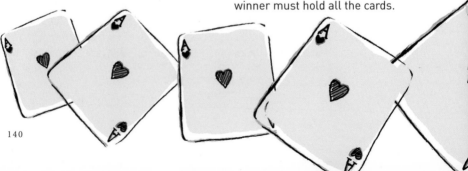

179

Build a house of cards

This needs patience, a flat surface, steady hands, no draughts and hopefully no sneezes.

Triangular house: Take two cards and balance the tips together at a point, like a roof truss. Continue until at least three trusses are side by side. Then place cards on top to form a roof/floor. Repeat the process of building trusses and floors until you have a single pair of cards at the top. The more cards you have, the higher your triangular house becomes or the more you can experiment with complex card structures.

Alternatively, use two cards on their sides, still as trusses but with additional cards at either end for stability. Then add extra trusses and build on top.

Handy hints...
For playing card games

KEEP THE SCORE

Be sure to keep a running score for all your card games. The overall loser at the end of play could be asked to do a fun family forfeit.

TOP TRUMPS

Play an alternative card game such as Top Trumps, whereby a player's card lists a series of statistics under a theme such as football clubs or sports cars that must beat – or trump – an opponent's card.

Games to play in the tent

180

It's choctastic!

Buy a bar of chocolate and give the kids a knife and fork. Set a short time limit and see how tricky the chocolate is to cut and eat (no picking up pieces with fingers allowed).

181

Look, no hands

Ever eaten jelly without hands? Put some chocolate buttons into a bowl and add jelly. Then try to eat the chocolate without using hands. Make it even harder using a blindfold.

182

Blindfolded feeding

Blindfold two people facing each other. Give them a bowl of tasty but messy dessert (think ice cream, jelly, squirty cream, pieces of cake). One person has to hold the bowl and spoon and feed their counterpart. Then swap places and get your own back.

183

Frozen peas

The humble bag of frozen peas can provide an array of games. Time how long it takes each player to transfer a pile of peas from one point to another using a drinking straw. Or create a marble run for peas (see page 143).

184

Cut the cake

Tip flour into a bowl, pack it down, place a plate on top and then invert the bowl and plate. Remove the bowl leaving a flour 'cake'. Carefully place a chocolate button or marshmallow on the top. Using a dinner knife, take it in turns to cut the cake into slices and remove them. The player whose cut causes the cake to collapse must eat the treat in among the flour without using their hands. Rebuild the flour cake and start the fun all over again.

185

Forehead detective

A pack of sticky note pads is needed for this game. Write down the name of a famous person, real or fictitious, on a sticky note and pass it to the player on the left without them seeing it. Everyone sticks their note to their forehead and the game begins. The person whose turn it is asks questions of the group to work out their identity. The replies from the rest of the players can only be yes or no. Count the number of questions it takes to get an answer or put a time limit on it. The person who works out who they are the quickest or with the least questions wins.

186

Marble runs

Before leaving home and as part of your rainy-day forward planning, collect together a number objects with which to make a marble run. Ideal items include empty toilet and kitchen towel rolls, cereal boxes, drinks cartons, especially those with screw-top lids (great to drop a marble into), sticks and twigs, paper rolled into funnels and tubes, and egg boxes. Groundsheets can also be shaped as channels. Build and decorate the marble run incorporating jumps and tunnels. No marbles? Then improvise with frozen peas (as already mentioned), conkers or acorns. Just let the imagination run wild.

187

Memory games

Place 20 objects from around the tent on a tray and cover them with a tea towel. Then reveal the contents for a limited time, say 20 seconds, while the players memorise everything. The tea towel is replaced and the umpire removes one item away from prying eyes. The tray is brought back and the tea towel lifted. The winner is the first person to shout out the missing item. Alternatively, make it progressively harder by starting with ten items and increasing each round with another five objects. Or start with a large number of items and each round reduce the amount of time to memorise the objects.

188

Cash counting

Gather a set of coins of varying denominations. Stand in a circle and pass the collection to each other behind your back without looking. Use hands to feel the size and shapes of the coins. Work out what coins they are and add the value together. At the end of the round, each player writes down the sum of the coins on a piece of paper. Everyone then declares his or her value to see who was correct.

189

Last to smile

How long can you keep a straight face despite other players' best efforts to make you grin? As soon as someone's face cracks, they're out. Last person to smile is the winner.

190

Charades

Simple animated fun. Is it a book, play, song or film? Ensure the younger ones get their chance to do some acting too.

191

Puppet shows

Get the kids to make up a story then act it out using puppets. Improvise with the puppet theatre by tying string between two points and draping tea towels over the top to make the stage curtains. Camping tables placed on their sides will provide a puppet stage.

192

The silence game

When all around you is getting noisy and fractious, play the silence game (the person that loses is the first person to make any noise). Watch peace descend, at least temporarily.

193

Umbrellas aren't just for rain

Turn an open brolly upside down, put it into the corner and take it in turns to see who can throw a ball into it. It's not as easy as it sounds.

Living History

194
Restore a ruin

Take a trip away from the campsite and visit some ancient ruins. Encourage youngsters to play the architect and restore them in their own mind. Or better still, sit in the grounds and draw a picture of the castle or building in all its former glory.

195
Explore a castle

Climb the cramped circular stairs in a castle tower (and hope no-one's coming in the opposite direction), watch a jousting tournament or peek into the dungeons and medieval torture chamber – if you dare.

196

Dress up the kids

They could be a princess or knight in shining armour for the day.

197
Re-enact the past

Battle re-enactment events can make for a full family day out. Participants happily share their knowledge with visitors, not just of battles and weapons but of day-to-day life such as food, cooking and tents from the era. Compare them with your modern-day camping experience!

198

Go underground

Castles and caves often go together so get on a subterranean guided tour. It will be full of legends, and maybe even bat colonies.

199
Get a bird's-eye view

Climb a church steeple or castle tower (count the steps along the way) to get a view of the surrounding area. Spot local landmarks and see if you can make out your tent at the campsite.

"Camping days are full days. If you are not eating or sleeping you are walking, or bathing or playing games or spinning yarns..."

Camping magazine (now called *Camping & Caravanning*), 1921

Get crafty with nature's palette

200

Make a camping craft kit

You've got a first-aid kit for camping trips. And a ready-made cooking kit with preferred utensils plus all your favourite herbs and spices. So why not make a camping craft kit that you always take away with you too?

HERE'S WHAT YOU NEED:

- String
- Straws
- Plasticine
- Scissors, including a pair with a serrated edge
- Ribbon
- Glue dots or glue stick
- Pack of googly eyes
- Paint and paint brushes
- Coloured wool
- Crayons (chunky and strong for bark rubbing, soft for leaf rubbing)
- Colouring pens and pencils
- Pipe cleaners
- Assorted scraps of colourful fabric
- Pencil, paper and rubber
- Empty jam jars, envelopes and carrier bags for collecting
- Small beach bucket
- Magnifying glass to closely examine detail
- Aprons for messy little ones (and clumsy parents)

201
A bit sticky

Sticks are great to use for art and crafts, and there is usually a bountiful supply on the ground. So create an entire family of stickmen and stickwomen complete with names and a pet dog.

Look out for interesting twigs with sprigs that resemble arms and legs (although they don't need any). Alternatively, wrap pipe cleaners around the body to create limbs. Grass, leaves or feathers can be tied or glued to the top for hair with different styles for mum and dad, of course. Stick googly eyes to the head, or draw small faces on paper, cut them out and glue them to the stick. Add scraps of fabric for clothing.

Plasticine is handy for making the stick family stand on their own two feet. Once the family is complete, think about making stick furniture with natural materials such as acorn cups, and even craft a tipi for them using one stick as the central pole and layering other sticks around it, fastened at the top. Just don't forget the door.

202
Driftwood boat

Weathered driftwood found on a beach comes in lovely shapes and often has a wonderful texture. Use a piece to represent the hull of a boat and connect a twig or driftwood mast to it, fastened with plasticine. Cut out sail shapes from scraps of fabric using serrated-edge scissors, glue them to the mast, and add small pieces of string for the boat's ropes (known as lines). Draw a funky design on another piece of fabric for a flag and attach it to the top of the mast.

203
Make a collage

Set the children the challenge of collecting a variety of natural materials from a list, ticking them off as they find them. Consider things such as daisies, pine cones, twigs and leaves (remembering to identify the type of tree at the same time).

Have a large clean sheet of paper to hand and glue or tape the objects down, or they can just be laid out on top of it. Try to recreate the scene outside the tent door using the foraged materials. Or make an imaginative 3D map of the campsite.

Take the collage a step further and use the materials to create a fish or ladybird shape. The fish's scales or fins could be made from a collection of cockle shells, for example. Or craft a ladybird from tiny stones painted red and black, with twigs for the antennae. Alternatively, find a bug-shaped pebble and paint it bright ladybird colours, adding googly eyes to help bring it to life.

204

Shells, stones and pebbles

They are easy to find and, with a little imagination, shells, pebbles and stones are great for arts and crafts. Themes such as words, animals and patterns work well.

Shells come in some lovely shapes, sizes and colours (whelks, mussels, limpets and cockles are commonly found on our seashores). Think about adding googly eyes and seaweed for hair to make a funky sea creature. Plasticine will hold it all together.

Stones and pebbles vary immensely too and are very satisfying to paint once clean and dry. They make a great canvas for miniature scenes and portraits, but their smooth, flat surface is also good for adding letters to for word games.

205

Written in stone

Try to find 24 flat pebbles, one for each letter of the alphabet. Once painted with letters they can be used to spell out messages on the ground. Take a photograph of your message, get it printed and turn it into a holiday postcard. "Dear Granddad, You were right about the weather..."

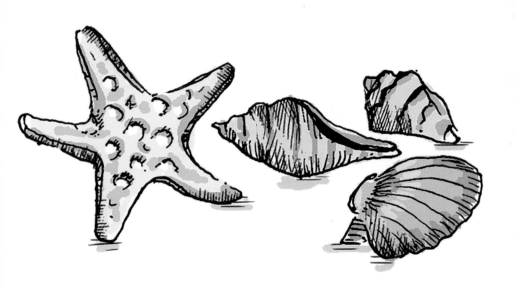

206

Rose petal perfume

To make your own fragrance, courtesy of Mother Nature, you'll need a small plastic bottle with lid or a clean jam jar (labels removed) to store the scent plus a couple of handfuls of rose petals, a sieve, pan and stove, and one-and-a-half to two cups of water.

First ensure the petals are clean. Then bring the water slowly to the boil. Add the rose petals and simmer for a couple of hours. Allow the water to cool, and then sieve the water. Give the now cool petals a squeeze in the sieve to remove further scent. Pour it into your bottle ready for use.

Dream up a name for your perfume and design a label to stick to the bottle.

Why not experiment with different scents by blending ingredients together? Try flower petals such as daisies and lavender, pine needles or even fruit.

207

Press flowers

Put the chosen blooms between two pieces of toilet paper and squeeze in a book for a week. Take them home and use to make postcards, as part of a picture or to decorate a homemade bookmark. Try seaweed instead for a keepsake of the beach.

208

Rub some bark

Look for interesting shapes in the bark and use strong, thick crayons to rub over paper pressed against the tree. Try using different colours on the same rubbing.

209

Design a duct tape bracelet

It doesn't sound like the most glamorous accessory but it's fun. Duct tape is popular with campers since it has multiple uses including repairing broken tent poles. Simply roll the duct tape loosely around the wrist, sticky side out. Then stick wild flowers such as buttercups and daisies, or colourful leaves and tiny stones, to the tape.

210

Paint with rain

Capture the raindrops in a beach bucket on a wet day and use that to paint with.

211

Make a daisy chain

Pick a bunch of daisies, all with nice long stems. Use your thumbnail to make a slit in one of the daisies' stems about midway down, through which you thread the stem of another daisy. Then cut a slit into that daisy's stem, and repeat until the bracelet or necklace is complete.

212

Take a leaf out of your book

Put a leaf on some newspaper, with the veins facing up, then place drawing paper on top. Carefully rub over the leaf in different directions with a soft crayon to reveal the pattern of the leaf's veins. Alternatively, paint the underside of the leaf and carefully press onto paper to get a print. For something a little messier, attach the leaf to paper. Dip an old toothbrush into paint and draw back the bristles. Take aim and rasp along the bristles towards yourself so the paint splatters in the opposite direction across the leaf and paper. Once the paint has dried, carefully remove the leaf to reveal a splatter picture.

213

Make a plaster cast of an animal's footprint

You'll need plaster of Paris (a small bag should do), water, a stick for mixing, and a strip of cardboard complete with tape or a paper clip to hold it in place.

Track down a nice animal footprint. Clear away any twigs or stones. Place the cardboard around the footprint in a circular shape, secured with tape to hold the ends in place. Mix the plaster of Paris with water and pour into the cardboard mould. Allow to set (it could take about 30 minutes). Pick up the now dry plaster of Paris, remove the card and reveal the shape of the footprint. It will be great for show and tell at school next week!

214

Draw a bug

Beetles and snails are interesting to look at. Carefully catch one and store it in a jar with the lid off. Use a magnifying glass to check out the detail, then get drawing. Set the little fella free once your masterpiece has been created.

Photography

215
Abstract nature photography

When the weather is good it's time to get out the camera and take some arty nature shots.

When choosing a theme, look for the detail and think both 'composition' and 'repetition'. For example, first pile up a mound of conkers still in their closed shells or husks and photograph them. Now mix in some conkers with split husks and snap again. Then remove the outer layer to reveal the deep brown colour and repeat the process.

216
Look for leaves

Leaves can make interesting subjects for photography, especially when light shines through the blade to reveal the veins and unusual patterns. Think 'seasons', too. Capture the leaves in spring or summer with their vibrant greens and yellows, then photograph the same type of leaf later in the year when autumn enriches them with shades of red and brown. Alternatively, gather together a nice big pile of fallen leaves and have someone kick them or throw them into the air for an action shot.

217

Pretty patterns

Look out for opportunities to photograph other types of nature's patterns. When it's feeding time, have you ever seen a herd of sheep converge towards the same place? Or noticed how animals such as sheep and cows tend to follow the same trail even when out on remote farmland? It's a natural pattern that makes for a good photo.

218

Cloud art

Look at the clouds – though not directly into the sun – and see if you can spot and photograph faces and unusual shapes.

219

Tree bark

Close-up photos of knots in tree bark can also reveal interesting features and abstract shapes.

220

Wildlife

Flowers are great to photograph, especially close up, to reveal the tiny parts and rich colour. Add in a humble bumblebee having a snack and you've got the ingredients for a memorable shot. But be patient – any wildlife photography takes time. And while you might be keen to catch a rare glimpse, not to mention a photo, of a deer, remember there's plenty of wildlife at your feet that's more likely to put in an appearance in the form of bugs and other colourful creatures.

221

Rapeseed oil crops

Set against a landscape of green fields, rapeseed crops can be stunning with their bright yellow colour. If you're out for a countryside walk, move to a different location and photograph the same field to see just how different it looks. Or revisit the same spot at different times of the day to get different light effects and to see what a change of weather can do to the setting.

222

Paint with light

Good photographers are really artists who know how to paint with light. Experiment with natural light and also have a play with the many settings on typical digital cameras to get some truly special effects.

223

The camping selfie

The 'selfie' is a recent social media phenomenon but the concept goes back way before the camera was invented. And it can be both fun and creative.

Selfie-sticks are often used to help cram in more smiling faces. But when used effectively, they provide a great opportunity to include background or context to the location.

224

Make them smile

This little trick is great for kids to try if they're struggling to get people to smile for the camera or want to make people laugh. Pose the group and then look through the camera's viewfinder. Hold the camera nice and steady with a finger on the shutter release button (the one that takes the pictures). Just as people are expecting the photo to be taken, keep the camera steady and in the same place but quickly move your head to one side and pull a big funny face, clicking continuously as you do so.

The results make for good, natural laughter shots.

225

Snapshot challenges

Devise a game whereby the children must photograph specific objects or places, a bit like a treasure hunt around the campsite. So challenge everyone to find and photograph something beginning with the same letter, for example, or the same colour. Or set an alphabet challenge. Start with the letter A and work through the alphabet. F for fox or friend, T for tap or tent peg, and X for, er, crossroad (some letters will require more creativity than others).

Set a snapshot challenge along the lines of a conceptual theme, for example Bat and Ball, Pyramid, Trees, Beasties or Water Carriers. Be creative to dream up your photo that illustrates the concept.

226

I-spy with my little camera

Disposable cameras can still be bought with children in mind and are quite inexpensive. They're ideal if you have a pricey digital camera but don't want young hands fumbling with it. And there's an added benefit.

Everything in modern-day life is so instant and fast that the results of a disposable camera are actually something to look forward to. You'll have to wait for the prints (remember those?) in excited anticipation. So buy a pack of disposable cameras, give one to each child with their names on (not forgetting Mum and Dad), and tell everyone they have just 24 frames to photograph their I-spy camping camera list. Here's mine based upon a young family:

- Funniest moment when pitching the tent
- Carrying water
- The weather
- The biggest smile
- My favourite moment
- A friendly furry animal
- The bestest bug
- The funkiest wellies
- Favourite meal.

When the prints arrive, gather the family around for a fun evening with prizes for the best in each category, as voted for by the whole gang.

227

Make a postcard

Whatever happened to sending postcards when on holiday? It's one of those things we just don't seem to do any more. Let's try to bring it back into fashion, though with a modern-day twist.

Simply upload your best photo to one of many websites that print and mail postcards, add your message and delivery address, pay the cost and it's off. You'll need an internet connection of course, but what a lovely way to say to Granny 'Wish you were here'.

228

Make a campsite photo album

In all reality, this will need to be done at home so that images can be printed off, and you'll need to buy a special scrapbook or photo album. The story can be told in chronological order, though it could also be created following themes such as people, places, activities, the campsite itself and local wildlife. Remember to include captions – always including the names of people, dates and locations – and get the kids to write down their feelings and views too, to make it a more personal record.

A photo album or scrapbook can be used to make a diary of a particular day. Set a maximum number of photographs to ten, for example, and capture the essence of that day from dawn until dusk.

Alternatively, take a more digital approach and upload images to a website that publishes photobooks, together with captions, and create one that way. The images can be cropped using the website's software to get the best look from photos. You'll be glad you did in years to come.

229
Go large

Digital images are easy to upload to photographic printer websites that can enlarge and turn them into posters. Provided you have a high-resolution picture file you can zoom in and crop a part of the photo for maximum impact.

I had two posters made from photographs of my son Tom doing his first multi-pitch climb with an instructor during a camping trip to the Lake District. I was watching from afar with my heart in my mouth as he made easy work of the rock face while a photographer friend expertly caught it on camera. Those photos now adorn Tom's bedroom walls as framed posters and I've lost track of the number of times I've stood and stared, just looking at the colour and detail of the enlarged images, and fondly remembering the moment.

230

Enter a competition

Proud of your pictures? Then enter a competition. There are plenty aimed at children and they often involve themes that are ideally suited to the great outdoors. Sometimes the best photograph is the least expected. Just get snapping.

231
Just for laughs

You've had a fun day with photography, now have fun at the expense of those in the frame. Download the pictures to a laptop, enlarge the best ones featuring friends and family and have a caption competition with a prize for the funniest.

232
Make a camping vlog

Most digital cameras and smartphones have the capability to film video clips, so why not make a camping 'vlog' (videolog)?

Before leaving home, ensure that the editing software, some of which is free, has first been downloaded to the smartphone or tablet device (the connectivity at home may well be better than the campsite's).

Kids will need a camera with them all the day, and every time they do something memorable or see something interesting (an unusual bug or a strange shape in the clouds perhaps), they film it and talk about it, expressing opinions and describing what's going on. Watch a few videos online at home first for inspiration. When editing back in the tent or caravan, think about chronological order and keep it short and interesting.

233
Make a nature documentary

Set out to find a certain type of animal – rabbits are frequent campsite residents and will often stay put until you get too close. Find out what's local to the campsite. Encourage children to research their chosen subject using books, the internet, apps or the adults around them.

Once the research has been done, why not draw a colourful storyboard before filming gets underway to use as a guide. Start small with more common creatures such as rabbits and robins before going in search of deer. And if the deer stays hidden, that could also make your documentary – 'My Search for the Elusive Deer of the New Forest'. Think about creating cinematic shots, so include the surrounding landscape and the nearby flowers and bushes to ensure the film has a sense of place. Consider setting it to music or adding narration that tells the story.

234
Become an interviewer

Children could take it in turns to record set pieces to camera or film interviews with people such as the campsite managers, asking them about the types of wildlife they regularly see on site.

235
Film at night

Don't forget that wildlife is quite different at night – think bats, owls, foxes, badgers and hedgehogs – as are the skills required to film successfully in the dark. Red lights on headtorches will preserve your night vision as well as helping to avoid startling any animals. If narrating, whisper to the camera – it will help prevent any animals knowing you're there and also give the film greater atmosphere and tension.

236
Time-lapse videos

These are relatively easy to make on a smartphone – provided you don't move it. Catch a sunrise or sunset, or the movement of clouds across a bright blue sky.

237
Action-cams

These can provide a very different perspective to your adventures given that you don't have to worry about holding them. They're brilliant at capturing the excitement of the moment and the footage can be used in its entirety or edited to become part of a documentary.

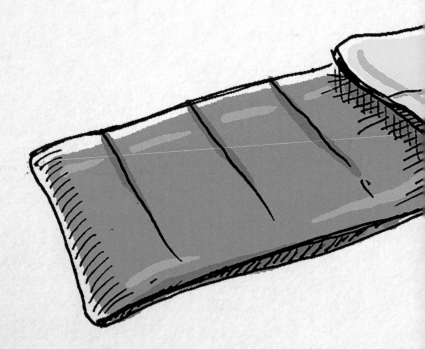

5

NIGHT-TIME FUN

> **" 'Our first night of camping,' thought Anne, happily.**
> **'I shan't go to sleep. I shall lie awake and look at the stars**
> **and smell that heathery smell.'**
> **But she didn't. In half a second she was sound asleep too."**

Enid Blyton
Five Go Off To Camp, Hodder & Stoughton, 1948

Life feels so much better after a good night's sleep. We're much more capable of dealing with whatever the day throws at us, including wet weather, if our batteries are fully charged.

Thomas Hiram Holding, founder of The Camping and Caravanning Club, once wrote: "Sleep is as necessary as food. After a good night's rest a good day's work is enjoyed. A more or less disturbed night makes a dull day... The best of all sleep provokers is fresh air and exercise."

Those words were published in 1908 and are still spot-on today. Just as you'd hope for a good night's sleep at home, a night under canvas should be no different. However, it's not always easy to achieve given your new-found surroundings. Mother Nature has a habit of reminding people they're in the countryside, usually just as their head hits the inflatable pillow.

You want to be bright-eyed and bushy-tailed to face the adventures ahead – and the whole family will be better for it. So how do you prepare for a good night's sleep? That can be answered in two words: warmth and comfort. Or perhaps three with the addition of light. But let's make it four: warmth, comfort, light and earplugs.

Warmth

A good night's sleep is so much easier if you're the correct temperature. I find it easier to wrap up warm and cool down by ditching a layer or unzipping my sleeping bag a little if I'm too hot rather than putting on clothes if I wake up cold.

Invest in the best sleeping bag you can afford and keep it clean to help maintain its lifespan. Sleeping bags have temperature and season ratings, so pick the one that best suits the time of year in which you'll be camping. They come in an array of shapes and sizes, and with features such as hoods (great for adding warmth), built-in lights and internal storage pockets.

The best way to get the most from a sleeping bag is to dress light and use an inner bag, which will upgrade the rating of the sleeping bag. If you haven't got an inner bag and it's cold, wrap up with layers of clothing if need be, though too many clothes may affect the sleeping bag's efficiency. Keep socks on and even consider wearing a woolly hat and gloves if it's really cold. How often do children get to sleep in clothes at home? It all adds to the adventure.

Comfort

What lies beneath your sleeping bag is important for comfort and also warmth, as the ground can chill you year-round. Self-inflating mats (often called SIMs) remove a lot of the puff required with airbeds. The layers between the camper and terra firma can be boosted with additional insulation such as thermal and foam mats. If you think about putting a blanket on top of you, think also about putting one underneath for added insulation.

Did you inflate the airbed earlier in the day in warm weather? If so, the chances are it will feel less firm come the evening due to cooler temperatures. So inflate it a little more just before bed. When you wake up, slightly deflate an airbed or open the valve of a SIM, if that's what you're using, to prevent them from potentially bursting in really hot weather. Alternatively, lift yourself off the ground completely with a camp bed. Modern versions are compact and lightweight, and some even allow you to sit on the end without tipping it up.

Night-time comfort calls may be a consideration. Caravans and motorhomes offer an obvious solution to that problem with their own toilets, so tent campers may want to consider having a portable loo in the porch section, just in case.

Light

If you're camping in a tent, as opposed to a caravan or motorhome, you're unlikely to have the convenience of a light switch to hand if you wake in the middle of the night and need to get up. It's amazing just how dark the countryside can be away from the neon glare of towns.

Light can be a security blanket at night, especially for children, so keep torches close to hand throughout the evening. When you go to bed, remember exactly where you put the torch. It's sensible to have spare batteries – and know where they're kept too. A wind-up torch is a good idea for forgetful (or completely worn out) kids who may leave them on all night. Head torches are great for all the family but children especially seem to like them. Many have a red night vision mode that's ideal for giving just enough light to see what you're doing without illuminating the entire tent in the middle of the night and waking everyone up. Modern battery or solar-powered lanterns have useful settings that can be used to dim the light at that point in the evening when children are settling down and the grown-ups want to stay up a little later.

People once woke up naturally with the sunrise. These days sunshine on a tent will brighten up anyone's day – but not necessarily at 5am. So eye masks may be the solution, or buying a tent with sleeping cabins made from darker fabric. More tent manufacturers are using darker materials to line the tent's sleeping cabins, which help block out the early morning sun. To exclude more daylight, try laying a sheet over the inner cabin.

Earplugs

The dawn chorus is a wonderful sound to wake up to. Birds are singing to attract a mate and defend their patch. And since the air can be still early in the morning, the sound of birdsong travels further, meaning it can get very noisy out in the countryside more than an hour before sunrise. So Mums and Dads should consider using earplugs if they want to sleep in longer.

Alternatively...

A peaceful night's sleep is high on most people's list of what helps make a good holiday, but sleeping outdoors offers so many opportunities for night-time fun that you might want to set aside at least one night for some nocturnal games and exploration. It's the stuff that makes a camping trip truly memorable and exciting for kids – a real taste of freedom and a break from rules and routine. Chances are they will talk about it for years to come!

Many children find it hard to comprehend that just when most of us go to sleep, much also awakens in the natural world around us. Night-time brings darkness and with it a touch of mystery and even fear of what is 'out there', unknown and unseen, especially for children. But exploring at night helps them to realise that the night is a vital part of our natural life and it's a fascinating time to be outside.

These days kids are much less likely to play outside after darkness falls, let alone go for a walk. Camping is a natural way to reacquaint us with the night and the perfect opportunity for little ones to enjoy the excitement of staying up after bedtime, safe in the family environment. The vast majority of campsites are in the countryside and that means away from the neon glare of urban life. One small step outside your tent or caravan and you're confronted by deep, all-embracing darkness. Gone are the street lamps of home.

Stargazing for kids

Sitting outside late at night staring up at the stars is one of life's oldest and simplest of pleasures. Trying to figure out constellations, scanning for shooting stars or hoping to catch a glimpse of the International Space Station can keep you busy for hours. Even if you're completely unsuccessful at any of those, it doesn't matter because you are there, in the moment, chilled out and in total awe of the beauty of our galaxy as it unfolds above you.

Stargazing has been enjoying a renaissance in recent years and it's a superb way to capture and excite the imagination of young minds. People have boundless curiosity and the cosmos is an endless source of fascination. Astronomy is also a cool way to get interested in science.

The artificial lighting of our towns and cities ensures that most of us will not regularly enjoy true dark skies, which means camping and stargazing were made for each other. Pitching up in the countryside provides the ideal time and place to leave behind the glare of the large connurbations and enjoy the cosmic show. You barely have to poke your head outside the tent or caravan to get an eyeful of the sky at night.

Seek out dark skies

The great thing about campsites is that they're largely away from built-up areas with bright street lighting. Look out for campsites in official Dark Sky Parks or Reserves. In the UK there are also more than 100 designated Dark Sky Discovery Sites. Search 'light pollution maps' online to find out the darkest spots nearest you.

Kit to use

In its simplest form, you don't need anything. Just look up to the night sky and let your eyes gradually adjust. As they do, more stars and planets will come into sight. A book or chart to identify stars and constellations will definitely help, as will one of the many and quite amazing apps for smartphones and tablet devices.

You can take stargazing a step further with a pair of binoculars or a telescope. A tripod will help stability and keep the lenses focused on a specific spot to study in detail and to share with others. A compass will give an accurate bearing when identifying stars. Winter's the best time for clear, crisp nights so wrap up warm. Red light torches will help prevent your eyes from having to readjust in the dark. Keep a log book. Record information such as the date, weather conditions, location and what was spotted.

Constellations

Constellations are groups of stars that form a recognisable shape or pattern in the sky, resulting in them having been given the names of mythological creatures or forms.

Orion is a well-known constellation that can be seen throughout the world. Meanwhile the zodiac constellations include Gemini (the twins), Taurus (the bull) and Leo (the lion). Ursa Major is the Great Bear and seven stars of the constellation at its tail end make up the Plough (known in the US as the Big Dipper). Identification of the Plough, which looks like a saucepan, can determine the direction of north. By using the two outer stars of the pan furthest from the handle, draw a line between them and it will point to Polaris, the North Star.

There are many interesting mythical stories and facts about the 88 constellations – choose a favourite and search for it in the sky. Also try to identify your own birth sign constellation from the zodiac group.

So fear not the darkness and step forth with the family into the nocturnal world on a journey of fun, intrigue and discovery – you can catch up on sleep tomorrow!

Sleep well

238
Calm it down

Settle down the excitement with a calm period before bedtime, and enjoy a campsite story or singalong (see pages 112–117).

239
Have a milky drink

Make a relaxing hot chocolate before bed. Check out the recipe on page 212.

240
Know your own tent

If anyone needs to visit the loo in the middle of the night, make sure the tent is identifiable from the outside – they are easy to lose in the dark when half asleep and bleary-eyed.

241
Tire them out

Remember the words of both Thomas Hiram Holding and Anne of *Famous Five* fame. Fill the day with fun – you'll be pleasantly worn out and sleep will find you.

242
Fun bedrooms and kit

Invest in some of the fun family camping accessories on the market to make bedtime more enjoyable, ranging from bedrooms with jungle patterns to funky sleeping bags and novelty head torches featuring animal faces.

243
Geese at five o'clock!

During the night the family may all have heard the same noises outside – snuffles and snorts of little mammals or midnight bird screeches. Or an incredibly noisy squadron of Canada geese flying in formation overhead early in the morning before making a synchronised splash landing.

Remember to chat about this the next morning over breakfast and reassure little ones that it's just the local wildlife getting themselves ready for the day ahead. Just like you are. It's also a learning opportunity. Can you identify that bird call? I bet if you ask the campsite staff, they'll give you the lowdown on the local wildlife.

244

Learn Morse code

Why say 'goodnight' when you can send night-time messages using

Morse code (see page 55) with torches? If the torch doesn't have a signal button or good enough on-off switch, use hands to obscure the light in dots and dashes.

-. .. --. .... -   -. .. --. .... -

('night night').

245

Zip it up (quietly)

When will someone invent the silent zip? Or if one exists, when will tent manufacturers start using them? It's amazing just how much noise a zip can make, especially in the middle of the night or early in the morning when you need to answer a call of nature.

I've tried to work out the best way to silently open a tent or awning door and therefore keep the campsite happily ensconced in the Land of Nod, but I've yet to succeed. The best I can suggest is to carefully place your fingers close to the pull-tab to muffle the sound as you slowly unzip the door.

Unroping a tent door as I did in my youth was so much quieter, if a little slower and definitely draftier.

Things to remember...

NO TREES PLEASE

Avoid pitching tents beneath the branches of trees. Not only can branches fall in bad weather, but if it's raining you're more likely to hear the drip of large droplets on the tent. Bird lime, sap and honeydew can also cause problems, as can lightning.

LIGHTS OUT AT 11

Many campsites expect people to settle down at 11pm. It's a good time to bed down for a decent amount of sleep if you're expecting the dawn chorus to be your alarm clock.

THE TOP END

If the ground slopes, sleep with your head at the top end to avoid waking with a headache the next morning. And don't forget your favourite pillow!

KEEP IT DOWN

Noise carries further in the quiet of night so be considerate to those around you who are trying to sleep.

Exploring in the dark

246
Sunset finger trick

Estimate how long until the sun sets using your fingers. Extend your arm fully and count the number of finger widths between the sun and the horizon. Each finger represents about 15 minutes, which means each hand width should be about an hour.

247
A walk in the dark

Start your night-time adventure by watching the sun go down. It signifies the end of the day, although yours is just beginning. Get local advice on the best place to see the sun set. It always looks spectacular across water as it reflects in the ripples. Then head out. It's best to pre-plan the route to avoid the chance of getting lost. Why not follow a marked woodland trail using torches to pick out the sign posts? You don't have to venture far and can easily retrace your steps. Along the way talk to the children about how their senses become heightened in the dark. Encourage them to 'tune in' to their new night-time surroundings.

248
Switch to red

Switch head torches to red light to help with night vision. Or avoid torches and allow your eyes to naturally adjust to the darkness.

249
Use your senses

Stop and be silent for a few moments to listen to the wildlife. Listen out for the bark or howl of a fox, the grunt of a badger or the 'twit-twoo' of an owl. Switch off your torch and feel the contours of bark on a tree. Focus on your sense of smell. Does that sense feel stronger because you're relying on it more? Encourage youngsters to describe the scents around them. Use breakfast time the following morning to talk about all the different creatures seen, heard and maybe even smelled.

250
Get a guide

Join a guided night-time or dusk-watch walk. Guides such as forest rangers are often eager to share their knowledge of nocturnal wildlife on badger-watching walks and the like. You're more likely to spot an animal – and less likely to get lost.

251
Gaze at stars

Find a clear spot, lay on a blanket and stare up at the stars in the night sky. As your eyes adjust, more will become visible. If you're lucky you might even see a shooting star (see page 175–179 for more stargazing tips).

Handy hints...
For a night-time walk

PLAN THE ROUTE
Allow considerably longer to complete a night walk than you would for a daylight one.

EXAGGERATE YOUR STEPS
When on rough ground, make your steps higher than normal to avoid tripping over.

TAKE A TORCH
Don't forget the torch. And some spare batteries. You want to avoid getting lost.

WEAR REFLECTIVE CLOTHING
This is especially important if you're walking on or near roads.

REMEMBER THE MAP
Take a map and compass with you (and have the knowledge to use them).

USE THE MOONLIGHT
Aim for a night walk with a full moon and a clear sky. It's surprising how much natural light it will provide.

252
Call an owl

Try blowing through cupped hands to mimic the sound of a tawny owl – a high percentage of males can be fooled into giving a response.

253

The starling murmuration

Okay, so it's not quite dark yet but one of the most incredible spectacles of nature to witness is the starling murmuration just before dusk. Thousands flock together above their roosts and take to the skies for a series of aerial acrobatics, creating the most amazing display of shapes. We've all seen on television the way fish swim together in shoals, changing direction in unison. Starlings have their own version as they swoop around the sky. I've been lucky to see a murmuration on several occasions above reedbeds close to where I live and it makes you stop and stare in awe. It's a wildlife show at its finest. And it's free.

The birds begin to form roosts in autumn but can start as early as September. The RSPB has a number of reserves where murmurations take place – go and see one for yourself.

254

Fun and games

On nights when sleep doesn't beckon, why not head out to the campsite playing fields, away from tents and caravans, for some evening entertainment with friends and family? You're on holiday, after all, so there's no reason why bedtime rules can't be stretched a little bit.

255

Play Firefly

One person is chosen as the firefly and is given a torch. They run off into the field while the rest count to 100 and then flash the torch. The other players set off in pursuit to tag the firefly who can then move about the playing area. However, as they do so they count to 60 and each time they reach it they have to flash the torch to give the pursuers a clue. The first person to catch the firefly takes the torch for the next turn. Remember to use hearing as well as sight.

256

Family tag in the dark

One person is 'it' and the rest of the players scatter in the field. Once a person has been tagged, the first person remains 'it' but is now joined by the person they caught.

As play continues, the group of pursuers becomes progressively larger until there's only one person left – the winner.

257

Torchlight Hide and Seek

A night-time version of this timeless classic kids game. Limit the amount of time a torch can be switched on (try a count to three) and instead get players to rely on their night vision and hearing. When they think they've tracked down the player, switch on the torch and catch them in the beam.

258
Glow stick tracking

Take a pack of glow sticks to camp and lay a trail that the trackers have to follow, collecting them up as they go.

259
Glow stick quoits

Push several sticks into the ground, each with a glow stick attached, and allocate them different point values based on distance. You could also bend glow sticks into hoops to make your own quoits.

260

Stage a shadow puppet show

Torches and tent sides were made for creating shadows. What's more, headtorches mean both hands are free to create the silhouettes and shapes. Everyone needs to join in with a story, including grandparents. Just don't forget the popcorn.

261

Tasks in the dark

When all the light has gone, people quickly realise how utterly they rely on it. Just ask anyone who has forgotten their torch on a camping trip and only realises it when they turn in to bed for the night.

To find out how important light is, set the family a series of seemingly simple challenges to complete in the dark that rely on other senses such as touch and sound. You could challenge them to:

- Tie a knot.
- Rethread shoelaces onto a walking boot.
- Transfer water from one bottle to another without spilling any.
- Draw what they think is in front of them and then get them to write their name at the bottom.
- Peel a potato without missing any skin or turning it into a chip.

262
Bat spotting

Sadly, bats are often misunderstood and thought of as something to be feared. It's a real shame as they're fascinating creatures despite their peculiar looks and unwarranted reputation as blood-suckers. Britain has 18 species and it's fun to spot them out hunting at night. Look between trees that are a reasonable distance apart and you'll stand a better chance of spotting a fast-moving black shape in the night sky. A bat detector will also help and these can be hired on some campsites. Bats build up a picture of their surroundings in the dark by using high-pitched calls called echolocation. A bat detector effectively converts these calls into something we humans can hear. The device can also help identify the species. The common pipistrelle is one species to look out for. It flies fast and in jerky movements as it hunts and eats its insect dinner mid flight – up to 3,000 of them in any one night.

Handy hints...
Bat-spotting tips

DO YOUR HOMEWORK
Read up on bats in advance of the holiday to better understand them and have an idea of the species to spot in the area around the campsite.

INCREASE YOUR CHANCES
Joining a bat-spotting walk and hiring a bat detector device will increase your chances of spotting a few of these elusive animals.

BE PATIENT
Remember to take a torch, keep warm and be patient (not to mention quiet – let your ears do some work).

263
Make a moth trap

There are some 2,500 moth species in the UK, some of which are often mistaken for butterflies. Despite most being nocturnal, they are attracted to light. There are more complex DIY moth catchers that are ideal for use in the garden. However, these two designs are simpler and therefore better suited to camping.

1. Hang out a square of white sheet over a branch and shine a strong torch on it, ideally with no other lights on nearby. Place empty egg boxes at the bottom as a type of roost into which the moths will hopefully head.

2. The second style is messier and smellier as it uses sweet scent to attract moths rather than light. Fill an old sock with rotted fruit and even soak it in wine, and hang it from a tree or line. Alternatively, cut strips of fabric, mix red wine with sugar and heat until the sugar dissolves. Once cooled, soak the fabric strips in the mixture and drape over branches.

Return to these moth catchers after a couple of hours and check out the little visitors who will be feeding.

Carefully coax specimens into a clear plastic tub to identify and photograph before setting them free.

To help record moth numbers and species, take part in a national moth count event such as Moth Night, the annual celebration of moth recording throughout Britain and Ireland.

264

Make a lantern

Need a bit more light at night in the tent? Well, making your own lantern couldn't be easier. Fill an empty plastic bottle, minus labels, with water. Strap a headtorch around the bottle with the light facing in. It's a simple and illuminating idea.

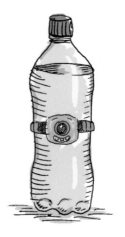

265

Make your own constellation

This is a great little art and craft idea that I remember doing at Scout camp when I was a youngster. Take a used cardboard roll and a piece of dark paper or tin foil. Place the end of the roll on the paper and draw around it. Within the circle copy the stars of

your chosen constellation by marking them with a dot, avoiding the edges. Use a pin to make a tiny hole on each dot. Then place back on to the end of the cardboard roll and secure it with an elastic band. Look through the roll in the direction of the light to see your constellation. Later when stargazing you can refer back to your own creation to see if you can spot the real thing.

266
Study the moon

The Earth's own permanent satellite is great to study since it's hard to miss. It also has the ability to set anyone's imagination running. Younger children can try to spot the 'Man in the Moon'.

There's plenty to see with the naked eye including the large flat grey areas called *maria* (Latin for 'sea'), although a pair of binoculars will enable stargazers to see much more, such as craters.

Learn about the moon's phases: full and new moons, a waxing crescent moon and a waning gibbous moon. Once youngsters have studied the moon, get them to draw a chart of it using as much imagination as they like, not forgetting the aforementioned permanent resident.

There's an endless supply of astronomical entities to look out for. Here are a few to spot:

JUPITER
Brown bands of gas running around the planet Jupiter, or the gas giant's four most visible moons.

ANDROMEDA GALAXY'S BRIGHT CORE
The galaxy is the furthest away object that can be seen with the naked eye (2.2 million light years away).

MESSIER 13 (M13)
The faint smudge of Messier 13 (M13), which is also known by the much more interesting name of the Great Globular Cluster and is found within the constellation Hercules.

PROXIMA CENTAURI
The nearest star to the sun is a mere four light years away (remember the sun is Earth's closest star). That's roughly 24,000,000,000,000 miles away, give or take a few. The Milky Way, our own galaxy, is more than 100,000 light years in diameter.

267

Spot a satellite

There are thousands of satellites orbiting the earth so why not try to spot a slow-moving one? The Hubble Space Telescope can also be seen by the naked eye.

268

Map out the stars

Try to create a map in your mind of the Milky Way by checking out an old star chart. Then go online and look up an interactive sky or star chart – you can search online for mind-blowing animations of the scale of the galaxy and beyond. Then have a go at mapping out your own.

269
The Northern Lights

You may be lucky enough to see *Aurora Borealis*, or the Northern Lights, a spectacular sight in which coloured lights shimmer and dance across the night sky. The natural phenomenon is initiated by the sun and involves charged particles striking molecules and atoms in our own atmosphere, ultimately causing the atoms to light up. The aurora can sometimes be seen in the UK and there are websites that tell you when the conditions are right for it to occur.

270
Help at your fingertips

There are a number of apps available for tablet devices and smartphones giving interactive tours of the night sky. Using one is like being given a guided tour by an expert astronomer who can explain what's overhead at any particular time of year. We live in a hi-tech world that's taken men to the moon – use some of the technology to discover more about the cosmos.

271
Shoot for the stars

Keep an eye out for shooting stars! They're not actually stars but meteoroids burning up as they fall into Earth's atmosphere.

Meteor showers take place all year round, but the majority occur between July and October and also November and December.

272
Hold a star-studded party

Celebrate celestial sights on site. If you're pitched up, hold your own stargazing party on a clear night. Glamp up the tent or caravan with some cosmic art and crafts to get you in the mood, put on some space-themed music, tell some mythical constellation stories and invite your campsite neighbours to join in the fun. Have some binoculars and a pile of thick blankets or camping mats at the ready so you don't get a crook in your neck and invite everyone to lie back and stare at the stars. Anyone for a moon rock cake?

273
Say goodnight to the stars

Make stargazing part of the kids' bedtime routine on the campsite. Check out the stars with a mug of hot chocolate before heading to bed. Keep that routine going when you get home by looking out of the window. Even if it's cloudy, there are still weather conditions to talk about.

274
Sign up to an astronomy club

Get together with like-minded stargazing enthusiasts by joining a local astronomy club. It's great to learn about the universe yourself but club members will be able to share their own knowledge and advice, help to identify night-sky sights and even lend out stargazing kit.

275
Join a stargazing event

With the growing popularity of astronomy as a hobby and the designation of more Dark Sky Parks across the country, more and more gatherings are being held to coincide with specific celestial events. You might want to join a gathering of astronomy enthusiasts to watch the Perseid meteor shower, for example, which can produce up to 60 meteors per hour. Planetariums are also great places to visit to really get bitten by the stargazing bug.

276
Snap the stars

Learn some of the basic techniques necessary for photographing the sky at night – it's quite a skill.

277
Go for a stroll

Pick a dark, clear night and head off with the family for a night-time walk. Find a comfy spot, sit down with a flask of tea and look up at the Milky Way in all its glory. What could be simpler or more magical?

278

Spot the International Space Station

The ISS is a fascinating subject for kids given that it is crewed by real-life astronauts. And budding young space cadets can spot it in the sky.

You'll first need to visit www.spotthestation.nasa.gov and insert your location details. That will then provide the dates, times and where it will appear in the sky, and where it will disappear from view.

Sightings take place a few hours before or after sunrise or sunset. This is the best time to spot the space station because the sun will be reflecting off the craft and be especially visible when set against the darker sky.

The website also lists the amount of minutes you've got to spot the ISS before it disappears below the horizon – you won't have long – and the height in degrees.

Part of the fun is to use your hand to work out how high in the sky you need to look. The horizon is zero degrees and directly above your head is 90 degrees. If you clench your fist, hold it at arm's length and rest it on the horizon, the top of your fist will be about 10 degrees, often the point at which the Space Station appears. It will then rise to its maximum height before disappearing.

The website also lists the direction to look using points on the compass. For example on a certain date and at a specified time, the ISS will be visible for four minutes, reach a maximum height of 77 degrees, appear at 10 degrees above west and disappear at 61 degrees east-south-east.

6

CLASSIC CAMPSITE COOKERY

> **"[Guides] love to feel responsible for the success of a meal, and it is much more thrilling to have achieved the cooking of a potato than merely to have been instrumental in removing its skin."**
>
> *Campcraft for Girl Guides,* 1953

Although most of us have barbecues and other pieces of equipment designed to make cooking at a campsite easy and convenient, there's still a lot to be said for trying a few dishes cooked in the traditional way over the campfire.

People have been cooking over fires for thousands of years. That means the modern oven is a relatively recent invention and campfire cooking knowledge has faded within a very short space of time. How many of us ever cook over an open fire? Would we even know where to start? It's time to relearn this wonderful skill.

I remember my eldest son Tom as a Scout trying to make a cooked breakfast using a tin foil parcel placed in the embers of a campfire. The sausage was cooked but anaemic in colour while the 'fried egg' just mushed itself around the other ingredients. Cooking in foil parcels is brilliant on a campfire but, as Tom discovered, you need to be picky as to what you put inside them... This chapter will give you lots of great ideas for easy, tasty dishes to try your hand with, top of which is the classic campfire treat known as s'mores.

Of course, camp cooking doesn't have to be over a campfire. Whenever I go camping with friends, family or colleagues from the Club, cooking is the one thing I consistently end up doing, especially at breakfast time. But I don't mind – in fact I rather like it. It's really nice to be up with the dawn chorus and light the stove to get the kettle on for that first cup of tea of the day. Sometimes preparing breakfast has just involved boiling hot water for a pouch of expedition porridge for my sons and me before a day in the hills. At other times it's been rustling up a full English breakfast for friends and family. One of my favourite starters to the day though can be found on page 196 – my friend Rachel's one-pan breakfast using chorizo, egg and cherry tomatoes. It's quick, simple and utterly delicious. I once cooked this on a camping trip for colleagues who couldn't stop the banter, all aimed in my direction of course. However, Rachel's delicious recipe managed to quieten them down, if only for a short while. Cooking breakfast for the rest of the campers also has the added advantage of someone else having to do the washing up. It's only fair!

Scrummy s'mores

They're gooey, very sweet and few people want to venture past eating two of them. But they're an absolute favourite with children, not just because of their scrummy sweet taste but also for the fun you have making them.

For the uninitiated, a s'more is a toasted marshmallow sandwiched between chocolate and two biscuits. They have enormous potential for creating your own concoctions and that's all part of the fun – dreaming up tasty combinations, limited only by your imagination and the ingredients you've brought with you to camp.

There are several theories as to the origin of the name s'mores. One is that it was first published back in 1927 as 'some mores' in the US Girl Scouts handbook *Tramping and Trailing with the Girl Scouts*. It was then shortened somewhere along the way. The original three ingredients are marshmallows, chocolate and Graham crackers, which are sweet. On this side of the Atlantic, we tend to use digestive biscuits. But whichever side of the Pond you're on, they're a winner every time.

Breakfast of champions

Breakfast time on a campsite is a great time to watch the world wake up around you as you plan your adventures for the day. That first mug of tea steaming in the cold air, the smell of fresh coffee and sizzling bacon. A new day in the great outdoors is ahead of you.

Cooking on a camping holiday can be as simple or complicated as you want to make it, though many campers, and 'tenters' in particular, tend to go the more straightforward route. And it's so easy to get children involved – they love to chop and mix food, to stir and pour, not to mention crack eggs, so encourage it.

The best bacon butty challenge

Bacon sizzling on a barbecue or frying on a stove early in the morning creates the quintessential smell of the campsite. It's an aroma that will leave a lasting impression on your children and stand the test of time, as it has with my sons.

A bacon butty sets you up for the day. It perfectly complements a mug of tea. And it's quick and easy to make. Yes, we all have different tastes and preferences, but it's important to get it right. When you think about it, there's a bewildering array of core ingredients and that means a multitude of bacon butty combinations. In the pages that follow, there are lots of tasty ideas to help the nation's camping families come up with the best bacon butty ever while on their camping holiday.

And once breakfast has been and gone, there are a few recipes and ideas in the following pages that will get you through the rest of the day. They are convenient meals that are easy and fun to make that will prove popular with hungry young campers – even the picky eaters among them.

A family feast

The beauty of camping is that if you take children out of their daily routine and away from their normal eating environment, you will find that even the fussiest of eaters can be transformed.

In my experience, camp cooking has a positive effect on picky eaters. Fresh air and activity sharpens the appetite. And when blended with a bit of fun and forethought, not to mention the chance to ditch the knife and fork, you can really improve your chances of making mealtimes fun and keeping hunger pangs at bay. So we've taken that further with some fabulous family recipes courtesy of Ali Ray, the Eat Local

ambassador for The Camping and Caravanning Club who's toured the UK and beyond these shores in her trusted campervan called Custard, seeking out great local produce to cook back at the campsite. And as a mum of two, Ali has managed to get her children to eat pretty much anything she puts before them. Even mussels and eel.

Ali believes that one of the beauties of campsite cooking is that the stress of the dining table has gone. You're now allowed to eat with your hands and have your plate on your lap – everyone is more relaxed. That means you can be a bit braver with what you feed to your offspring because, put simply, they'll be more distracted and more hungry. It's all about getting creative with your serving ideas. Believe it or not, along with a roll of trusty tin foil, a bag of wooden skewers is one of the most essential pieces of kit for any family camping trip, as are tortilla wraps (you can pretty much put any food in them and kids will eat them). If the kids won't eat from a plate, roll the food up or push it onto a stick and it seems to change the whole dynamic. In this chapter, you'll find recipes that will allow kids (and mums and dads) to get ultra-creative when it comes to building plate-free meals on a stick or in a wrap.

Delicious dishes from yesteryear

It's frightening how much we stand to lose if we don't pass knowledge and skills down through the generations. It seems we share that knowledge less and less these days. Just as we want to 're-wild' a generation, let's also 're-skill' them by sharing that old-fashioned know-how.

Grandparents are great at this and none more so than my sons' grandma, Linda Neale. She was a Guide Leader for decades and over those years amassed a fount of knowledge about camping with kids. That meant building campfires, running camp kitchens, cooking for the hungry masses, ensuring everyone did their fair share on the duty rota, and teaching traditional campfire songs to successive generations of Guides. Grandma cooked delicious, healthy meals for hundreds of hungry mouths over all manner of stoves and campfires, while showing youngsters how to do it for themselves. Since we all love a good pud, this chapter gives you some of Grandma's old-fashioned campsite recipes for delicious yet simple desserts. Don't forget to keep those traditions and skills alive and kicking.

Pick your own

When you're camping, the goodness of Mother Nature's larder is often on your doorstep. It's easy and fun to learn how to identify and pick the fruit from wild blackberry bushes, mostly found in hedgerows, for a tasty treat. Kids love picking (and eating) them and you can't get fresher.

The ultimate hot chocolate

Those of us who were Scouts or Guides will fondly remember being given a steaming hot cup of cocoa around the campfire at the end of a busy day. It was the perfect way

to wind down as the temperature dropped with the setting of the sun. It signified an end to the action-packed daytime rota of the campsite as everyone prepared to settle down to a peaceful night's sleep. These days cocoa is often replaced by the many slightly more decadent versions of hot chocolate powders available to take away on camping holidays, meaning that this comforting nightcap is always quick and convenient to make. With our recipe on page 212, topped with luscious sweet treats, the kids get to mix and create their perfect bedtime drink – it's the most magical campsite night-time in a mug.

Thirst for adventure

Talking of drinks, children sometimes forget how important it is to take in enough fluids to keep hydrated during the day, especially when they're busy playing. And whereas plain water isn't terribly exciting, creating your own kid-friendly campsite cocktails can be the best fun ever. They are also extremely easy to make – and healthy too. The ideas at the end of the chapter focus on recipes for refreshing cold drinks that are bursting with seasonal soft fresh fruits that can be gathered free from the hedgerows or Pick-Your-Own farms. There's even a pattern for making your own paper cup to drink them in, should you run out of cocktail glasses...

Handy hints...
Cooking over a campfire

CUT THE TURF
Carefully cut out the turf where you plan to light your fire and roll it up. An area about a metre square should be fine. Once the fire is extinguished and no longer needed, replace the turf. If the campfire is being used for several days, store the turf out of direct sunlight.

REMEMBER THE EMBERS
Cook over the embers, not the flames. This means the campfire will need to be well established and with constant heat (ideally you want all your wood to have turned to hot embers), so plan ahead to avoid delays – hungry kids can get really grumpy. Fast.

USE A RACK
Put your pans on an old oven rack that's been placed level on two bricks, as it will be much more stable than pots being placed directly on to the fire. Likewise, a grill pan grid on top of bricks or rocks is a good way to cook meat and vegetables such as corn on the cob or peppers sliced into large pieces. If you use logs to support the rack instead of bricks, douse them with water regularly.

FAT NOT OIL
Cook with solid vegetable fat, especially in frying pans, instead of oil, which can easily catch fire.

Things to remember...

COLD WATER
Have a bucket of water to hand for minor burns or just in case the campfire starts to get out of control.

TIE IT BACK
Tie back long hair – you don't want that getting in the way.

GET SOME GLOVES
Use proper oven gloves, as tea towels just aren't up to the job.

SEEK PERMISSION
Don't forget to get permission for campfires. Make quite sure that the campsite or landowner allows them. Many campsites, including Camping and Caravanning Club sites and Camping in the Forest sites, do not allow open fires.

279

Grandma's corned beef hash

Here's a classic meal for four from 'back in the day'.

Peel and boil enough potatoes to make mash for four, remembering to season well. Set to one side.

Empty the corned beef from a 340g can and break it up with a fork.

Mix the corned beef with the mash and if it's too dry, add a beaten egg.

At this point you can add more ingredients including leftovers. Peas, tinned sweetcorn, finely chopped peppers, chopped onion or tomato – anything tasty. A deseeded finely chopped chilli will add some heat.

Divide the mix into four and, using your hands (ideally dusted with flour), shape into four patties each about 1cm thick.

Heat some vegetable fat in the frying pan (oil can quickly flash when over-heated) and then add the patties. Cook until browned on one side (about five minutes) and then flip over for another five minutes. Serve golden brown and enjoy.

280

Grandma's omelettes

Omelettes can be sweet or savoury and are delicious either way .

Allow at least two eggs per person. A fish slice or palette knife are useful utensils to stop the omelette sticking and to flip them over with. And Grandma recommends you always rinse an egg pan in cold water before washing up.

281

Sweet omelette

Beat two eggs in a bowl. Melt a knob of butter in a frying pan and add the eggs. After a couple of minutes, when the eggs have set, add some pick-your-own fruit such as raspberries, blackberries and strawberries down the centre. Then fold in the sides of the omelette onto the fruit and cook for a few more minutes.

282
Savoury omelette

As with the sweet omelette, beat two eggs in a bowl.

Add to the bowl your savoury ingredients, such as finely chopped peppers (a mix of red, yellow and green looks appealing), spring onion, peas, tinned sweetcorn and sliced mushrooms. Or use leftover food, which is great for omelette fillings. Season well.

Melt a knob of butter in the frying pan and add the egg and veg mix.

Cook for a couple of minutes until setting well. Flip the omelette to cook evenly (it will need a few more minutes) and to lightly brown.

283
Grandma's baked apples

Core some apples and fill the holes with sugar, sultanas or mincemeat, and golden syrup or honey. Wrap the apples in tin foil.

Bake in the embers of the fire (turn after five minutes) until they feel soft to squeeze (about 10 minutes). Allow to cool slightly but eat while still warm and sticky.

284
Foiled again

Tin-foil parcels are brilliant for campfire cooking, and work with both sweet and savoury ingredients. Make sure you take a roll of foil on your camping holiday.

285
Jacket potatoes

It's a classic. Wrap potatoes in foil, place in the hot embers (putting more embers on top) and cook for at least 45 minutes, depending on the size of the spud. Once cooked through, slice open and add the topping of your choice – butter, mayo, tuna or baked beans. Given the spud's skin, and foil parcel, jacket potatoes are great just to spoon out and eat. For an alternative recipe, cut slices into the top of the potato, though not right through to the bottom, and add slices of onions with butter.

286
Corn on the cob

Remove the outer leaves and lay the cob in some tin foil. Add seasoning and a good blob of butter. Fresh herbs such as thyme work well too. Roll the corn in foil and cook in the embers for up to 10 minutes, turning regularly.

287
Crumble in a package

Make a tin-foil parcel. Add a mix of ingredients such as rhubarb and strawberry, apple and cinnamon, or apple and chocolate, and a splash of water. Place in the embers of the fire and cook for a few minutes (about three minutes for rhubarb and strawberry, while apple and cinnamon would need approximately eight minutes). Open up and fold the edges of the foil down to create your own bowl. Then crumble good-quality ginger biscuits into each parcel, add a blob of crème fraîche and spoon straight from your makeshift bowl.

288
Sweet peaches

Cut the peaches in half and remove the stones. Add a blob of butter, a teaspoon of sugar (the two will caramelise) and a sprinkling of cinnamon in the middle. Wrap in foil and cook for about 20-25 minutes, turning regularly.

289
Nacho feast

Place nachos into a foil parcel with cheese and sliced jalapeño peppers. Seal up the parcel and heat in the embers until the cheese melts (it should only take a few minutes). Open the parcel and add dollops of sour cream, salsa and guacamole.

290
Fruit skewers

These are easy to make and very tasty. If you are using wooden skewers, soak them first for at least 30 minutes to avoid them catching fire. Good fruits to cook are bananas, pineapple, peach and apricot. Drizzle with honey, maple syrup or even melted chocolate.

291

Make some dough

Here's a fun and easy campfire treat for kids – the dough stick. And we've also got an Ali Ray recipe for a dough stick with a twist! The dough is easy to make at home and transport to your campsite. The best way to prepare the sticks is to use a sheath knife to strip the bark. Use non-toxic wood like hazel for utensils.

You'll need:

250g plain flour
250g strong white bread flour
1 tsp dried bread yeast (the boxes of individual sachets are really convenient
and each sachet contains 3 tsp yeast)
1.5 tsp salt
1 tbsp oil
325ml warm water

The dried ingredients can be mixed in a sealed freezer bag at home ready to be taken away.

1. Put the flour in a bowl, add yeast and the salt, and mix it with your fingers.

2. Make a well in the centre then add the oil and warm water.

3. Mix it all together with your fingers until you have created a warm, silken and springy dough.

4. Put the dough back into the bowl, cover it with a damp tea towel or cling film and leave it to rise for an hour.

5. Place the dough on a floured chopping board and knead it for five to ten minutes. To do this, use the ball of your hand to squash the ball of dough, then push it away from you to stretch it. Pull it back into a ball, quarter turn it and repeat the process continuously.

6. Break off a chunk of dough and roll it into a long piece that's not too thick. Then roll it several times around the stick (enough times so that it doesn't fall off), sit by the campfire and toast away, turning occasionally until cooked through. You'll know when it's ready by breaking off a piece of the end to see whether the centre is still doughy (it shouldn't be).

292

Dough stick with a twist

Shape a piece of dough around the stick so that it looks like a tube. Toast on the fire and when cooked, slide it off the end. Then cram it full of fresh berries (remember to pick your own) and enjoy. It's quite messy but deliciously fresh.

293

Flatbreads

The dough recipe (left) can also be used for flatbreads that can be cooked on a pan or griddled on the fire. Just divide the dough into four balls, then flatten and stretch each one with your hands until about 4mm thick.

Rub a little olive oil on both sides and pop in a pan over the fire for about five minutes each side. Then add your own toppings – garlic butter, houmous, chopped tomatoes with fresh herbs... Or wrap them around a sausage that's slathered in mustard and ketchup for your own tasty campfire sausage roll.

294

Orange cake

You need one large orange per person plus a packet of chocolate sponge or chocolate brownie cake mix (don't forget you'll need eggs and water too with these mixes). Add toppings to taste, such as broken-up chocolate buttons or small pieces of honeycomb, crème fraîche, ice cream sauces or squirty cream.

Cut off the top of the orange, keeping it to one side, and scoop out the flesh. The best way to do this is to run a knife around the edge between the flesh and the skin and then scoop the orange segments out with a spoon (you can eat them as they are not needed).

Make up the chocolate sponge or brownie mix as per the instructions and spoon it into the orange shell, though don't fill the orange right up to the top as the cake mix will expand during cooking. Replace the orange's lid and double wrap in foil. Place in the embers and turn regularly to ensure the orange cakes are cooked throughout. They should take about 30 minutes but may require longer, depending on the heat of your fire. Then open the foil, remove the lid, add your toppings and spoon out straight from the orange, which will have flavoured the cake.

295

Classic s'mores

S'mores are simple and delicious. Take two digestives and place a square of chocolate on both biscuits. Spike your marshmallows (maximum of two) onto a skewer or stick. Toast them over the campfire or barbecue, ideally turning them until hot and they start to brown. Place them onto the bottom half of your biscuit and chocolate and add the identical top layer. Push down so the hot marshmallows begin to melt the chocolate and, using that same pressure, remove the skewer (remember the marshmallows will be very hot, especially in the middle). Give the s'more a little more time to melt the chocolate and also cool down – and then scoff! They're messy to eat and the marshmallow sticks to your fingers and clings to your chin, so just go with the flow – there's no elegant way to eat one. S'mores don't have to be toasted on a campfire. Gas stoves will also do the job but the heat will be a lot fiercer.

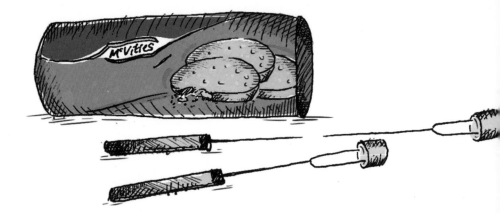

296

Our star s'more

It's easy to recreate the flavour of a banoffee pie. Just spread caramel sauce on both biscuits, then top with thinly sliced bananas. The hot marshmallows go in the middle as usual. The recipe tastes surprisingly close to the real thing.

297

Day to remember

In the US, and also more recently it would seem, Canada, 10 August is National S'mores Day. Write it in the calendar and start celebrating a classic campfire treat this side of the Atlantic. And let's give Trick or Treat, that other American import, a run for its money.

....

> "Toast two marshmallows over the coals to a crisp gooey state and then put them inside a Graham cracker and chocolate bar sandwich. The heat of the marshmallow between the halves of chocolate bar will melt the chocolate a bit. Though it tastes like 'some more' one is really enough."

Tramping and Trailing with the Girl Scouts,
1927

....

Handy hints...
S'more recipes

Marshmallows are the staple part of a s'more but the rest of it is wide open to interpretation and culinary invention.

VARY THE BISCUITS

Try malted milk or ginger biscuits. And instead of chocolate chunks, use chocolate digestives (the chocolate melts quickly). Chocolate Hobnobs are even tastier.

SWAP THE CHOC

Consider an alternative to chocolate such as jam, caramel sauce, peanut butter, honey and chocolate hazelnut spread. We've even tried cold custard (it wasn't great).

GOOEY COMBOS

- Malted milk biscuits (popular in our taste tests) with peanut butter and chocolate hazelnut spread.
- Lemon curd spread on the biscuits (no chocolate) for a lemon meringue s'more.
- Malted milk biscuits with strawberry jam and chocolate hazelnut spread.
- Ginger biscuits with caramel sauce and golden syrup (it's very sweet).
- Malted milk biscuits with caramel sauce.
- Lastly, what the heck, go healthy! Fruit such as raspberries and strawberries fresh from a pick-your-own farm are equally delicious extras.

298

One-pan breakfast

Here's a really simple, quick yet tasty one-pan brekkie that also works for lunch. A good friend Rachel Clark taught me this one and it's become a firm family favourite. I've also cooked this for friends on campsites and you know it's a success as the conversation stops while people tuck in. You'll only need one pan, ideally non-stick.

This breakfast feeds 4

You'll need:

200g Spanish chorizo ring cut into slices and halved

2 fresh, yolky free-range eggs per person (reduce to one for little ones).

Crack them into a separate bowl and beat with a fork

A handful of cherry tomatoes, halved

Fresh loaf such as tiger bread to serve

1. Get your pan on the stove and briefly heat without adding any oil. Add the chopped chorizo (the pieces should sizzle immediately) and cook for a few minutes until the distinctive red oil runs in the pan.

2. Add the eggs and the cherry tomatoes. Stir continuously and make sure the eggs do not stick, as they will cook quickly. The eggs will only take a few minutes to cook and once they look scrambled, remove from the heat (they will continue to cook in the pan).

3. The eggs pick up the distinctive flavour and colour of the chorizo oil. You can also add fresh parsley or coriander, and even swap the tomatoes for mushrooms, though I like the sweetness the cherry tomatoes bring to the dish.

4. Serve with slices of fresh tiger bread and a big mug of tea.

299

Ali Ray's sunshine hash

Ali Ray, The Camping and Caravanning Club's Eat Local ambassador, is a big hash fan because it's the perfect campsite brekkie. You can push the boat out or keep it simple. The hash can be made with leftovers from last night's meal or whatever you can get your hands on in the campsite shop.

This recipe for a good basic hash serves 4 generously

You'll need:

4 sausages
3 tbs olive oil
800g new potatoes, scrubbed and cubed
8 rashers of streaky bacon, roughly snipped or chopped

4 large ripe tomatoes, chopped
4 spring onions, chopped
4 large free-range eggs
Clove of garlic, chopped finely (optional)
Salt and pepper

1. Over a medium heat, cook your sausages in a deep, heavy frying pan. Then remove from the pan and put to one side.

2. Put two tablespoons of olive oil into the frying pan over a low/medium heat. Cook the potatoes for 15 to 20 minutes until they have turned golden in colour.

3. Add the pieces of bacon and cook for a further five minutes.

4. Add the chopped tomatoes and cook until they just start to soften. Stir in the chopped spring onions and garlic if using. Then add the sausages (you can slice them thickly before adding to the pan). Season well with salt and pepper.

5. Push the hash to one side of the pan and add another tablespoon of oil. Crack two eggs in the space, and fry until they are cooked to your liking.

6. Serve the hash between four plates, pop an egg on top of two of them, then return the pan to the heat and fry the remaining eggs for the last two plates.

7. Serve with tomato ketchup and big mugs of tea.

Handy hints...
Making a hash of it

You really can let your imagination run wild depending on your mood or whatever leftovers you have. It also makes sense to cook more potatoes than you need for an evening meal so you have a supply to use in your breakfast hash the next day. And if they are already pre-cooked, you don't have to fry them for as long.

VEGETARIAN VARIATION
Instead of the bacon and sausage, add baked beans and sweetcorn just before you cook your eggs, so they have time to heat. You can dry fry cubes of halloumi cheese (the squeaky stuff) instead of the sausages at the beginning or simply sprinkle the cheese on at the end of cooking.

BUBBLE AND SQUEAK HASH
Fried dark greens, such as kale and cabbage, with crispy bacon and a splash of soy sauce, work well. Add a handful of chopped cabbage at the bacon stage of the basic recipe on page 197, and leave out the tomatoes. It's salty, crunchy and filling.

GARLIC MUSHROOMS
You've got to fry them in butter to get the best effect here and ideally use those big field or Portobello mushrooms with the delicious dark gills that combine with the butter to make a gorgeous juice. So instead of using the sausages in the main recipe, you could slice up four large mushrooms and fry them in butter with lots of black pepper and a sliced clove of garlic. Take them out and put them to one side then follow the rest of the recipe.

SPICY HASH
Use sliced chorizo in place of the sausage and add half a finely chopped red chilli along with the bacon. If younger ones are less keen on spice, swap the chilli for a dollop of mild sweet chilli sauce.

300
Hold a toast topping competition

Get creative! Who can invent the best combination of breakfast toast toppings? Jars of Marmite, peanut butter, jams and lemon curds are easy to take on camping trips. How well do they go together? Or introduce some unusual cooked bacon combos.

Bacon with honey or maple syrup is popular in the US, or how about bacon with thinly sliced apple? Ever eaten mushrooms fried in butter and a teaspoon of Marmite? Now's the time to try it. And what delicious savouries can you match with marmalade?

Just ensure you have an 'independent' judge (grandparents are good at this).

301
Breakfast wraps

There's a theory that says kids will eat anything if it's in a wrap. My sons bear this out. They turn up their noses at the sight of something on a plate but put it into a tortilla wrap and suddenly it becomes palatable, even fun. Wraps have been a staple part of the McGrath family diet for years now.

Try smoked salmon slices and scrambled egg with fresh or dried herbs or a few capers.

Alternatively, you could do the same thing with scrambled eggs but put sundried tomatoes and goats' cheese along the middle, then spoon the egg over. How about a classic BLT? Crispy cooked bacon, a sprinkling of watercress, rocket and spinach (those bags of pre-washed salad leaves are great for a campsite), and thinly sliced fresh tomato.

Or if the kids even turn up their nose to Rachel's lovely chorizo, egg and tomato dish, spoon that into a wrap too! Once made, you can also fold up the tortilla and put it back in the pan to lightly brown on each side.

. . . .

"Mmmmm... Bacon"

Homer Simpson, *The Simpsons*

. . . .

302
Eggy bread

This is also known as French toast and is simple and fun, not to mention messy and therefore great for kids. I think white bread is best for this.

Beat four eggs in a bowl. Bring the frying pan up to heat with a little oil or butter. Dip a slice of bread into the egg and pop it straight into the frying pan. Fry for one to two minutes on both sides until the egg is cooked. Good with a dollop of ketchup.

As an alternative, coat the bread with cinnamon and sugar. Simply sprinkle some caster sugar and a little cinnamon onto a dinner plate and, once the eggy bread is cooked, press both sides down on the plate to coat it with the sugar and spice.

303
Posh French toast

How about a deluxe version of French toast? Butter the bread with a hazelnut and chocolate spread, and dip the slices into beaten eggs mixed with 10ml of double cream. Then fry in butter. You can also coat both sides with a caster sugar and cinnamon mix, as before.

304

The best-ever bacon butty

It's the classic campsite breakfast – and it comes in many combinations.

First consider the bacon. Do you want back, middle or streaky? Free range and organic? Smoked or unsmoked? Bacon can be cooked so it's juicy or crispy or even burnt. Should the fat be cut off and at what point? And how many pieces of bacon per sandwich?

Then there's the bread. White or brown? Packet or freshly baked? How about rolls and baps, or sourdough? Consider the thickness of the bread or the crustiness of the roll. And although I would never toast the bread on a bacon butty, some people like to put it lightly on the grill to give it some sear marks, giving it a hint of crunch.

What about the spread? It's a question of butter versus margarine. Should you even use a spread or allow the bacon fat to self-baste the slice?

Next come the sauce options. Tomato ketchup or brown sauce? Or even barbecue or sweet chilli sauces? And what about including any 'extras'? First and foremost that would have to be a fried egg, though tomatoes are also a good fit. How about something a little more exotic – avocado anyone?

And so the recipe for my best-ever bacon butty is... Free-range, organic unsmoked back bacon, fat removed after cooking, and not too crispy (if your budget allows, go for quality all the way). The bacon is sandwiched by hand-cut fresh tiger bread (I like the flavour and crunchiness of the crusts), not too thick, and lightly buttered. There are three slices of bacon in my sandwich (I'm on holiday after all). Quality brown sauce accompanies it, though I'd happily settle for tomato ketchup. Use sparingly to avoid overwhelming the other flavours.

If I wanted a larger breakfast, I'd add a runny fried egg (with kitchen towel at the ready). As a special touch, I would include ripe avocado and black pepper. With its creamy texture the avocado is nice for children, though they may want to give the black pepper a miss (and it's either an egg or avocado – never both). I would wash it down with tea, never coffee.

So there you have it: my best-ever bacon butty. The perfect campsite breakfast.

305
Full-of-favourites frittata

Here's another recipe from Ali Ray, The Camping and Caravanning Club's Eat Local ambassador. The frittata can be sliced, stored in a cool box and served for lunch.

This frittata serves 4

You'll need:

300g summer veg: broad beans, courgettes, asparagus, peas and spring onions or sweetcorn, peas, ham and cherry tomatoes, chopped
½ large red onion, chopped finely
3 rashers of smoked bacon cut into small pieces

300g cooked new potatoes, sliced
Fresh parsley and coriander, chopped
6 large fresh eggs
Salt and pepper
Grated hard cheese such as Cheddar (optional)
Salad leaves to serve

1. Put your chopped veg (except spring onions and red onion) in a pan of boiling water. Bring back to the boil then reduce the heat and simmer for three to four minutes until tender. Drain.

2. In a large frying pan, sweat the red onion and spring onion in a little oil for about five minutes.

3. Add the bacon after about two minutes then let it fry for a couple of minutes. Add the drained vegetables, cooked potatoes, parsley and coriander. Toss it all together and turn the heat down low.

4. Beat the eggs with salt and pepper and pour over the vegetables. Cook gently on a low heat and don't stir.

5. When the egg is nearly set (you can sprinkle on some cheese now if you want), put the pan under the grill for about five minutes until it has set. If you haven't got a grill, cook the frittata until the top has almost set completely. Cut down the middle with a spatula, slide one half out of the pan and put on a plate. Flip the remaining half over in the pan, and let it cook for about a minute. Then do the same with the other half. Slice into wedges and serve with salad leaves.

Handy hints...
Combine eggs and veg for a perfect brunch

A CAMPING STAPLE

Eggs are a camping staple, not least because many of the independent and smaller campsites are located on farms with a supply of fresh free-range eggs on the doorstep.

NATURAL GOODNESS

The summer camping season also brings with it an abundance of fresh produce. It's the time when fruit and veg take centre stage and flaunt their natural goodness wherever you turn. Farm shops and farmers' markets come into their own as a wealth of courgettes, aubergines, broad beans, peas, lettuce and tomatoes can fill baskets for pennies not pounds. And don't forget excess allotment veg can be picked up for a small donation into honesty boxes perched on gateposts.

FREE RANGE

The bright sunny yellow colour and wonderful flavour of eggs from chickens that have foraged in the open and have fed on food scraps make all the difference to a great frittata, which takes advantage of the glut of summer vegetables too.

Things to remember...

OIL THE BARBIE

Stop the bacon sticking to the barbecue by adding a small amount of cooking oil to a piece of kitchen towel and wiping it across the grill.

KEEP IT OUTSIDE

Never take a barbecue into a tent, awning, caravan or motorhome. Even a cooling barbecue gives off poisonous carbon monoxide (CO), which can kill. Stoves and barbecues are designed for cooking not space heating.

306
Easy-peasy pizzas

These are incredibly simple and fun to make with the children – ideal for the campsite. The key is to use tortilla wraps. Squeeze a good dollop of tomato paste from a tube onto the wrap, and spread it around. Sprinkle with grated cheese and dried herbs (mixed herbs are good here or oregano). Get the children to dream up the toppings, though you won't go far wrong with pineapple and ham. You could try cheese down one half and something savoury on the other side. What about goats' cheese and honey? Or indeed Marmite and mushrooms? Cook the easy-peasy pizzas in a dry frying pan. Once cooked, cut into quarters – and enjoy.

307

Brilliant burgers

Here's a recipe for home-made burgers that I've been using for years and love. It contains chilli and that means it might not be ideal for children, but there are easy ways around that to make a kid-friendly version that will be enjoyed by grown-ups too. There's lots of chopping and mixing to do, and that's always good to get children involved with, although you may want to chop the chillies yourself.

This is a burger full of flavour so try to avoid the temptation of adding too many extras or overloading it with ketchup.

This recipe serves 4

You'll need:

650g minced beef
1 garlic clove, finely chopped (optional)
1 red pepper, deseeded and finely chopped
1 red chilli, deseeded and finely chopped

1 tbsp fresh basil (1 heaped tsp if using dried)
½ tsp powdered cumin
Salt and pepper

1. Put the mince into a mixing bowl and add the garlic, red pepper, chilli, basil and cumin. Season well with salt and pepper. Mix thoroughly, then break off burger-sized quantities and form into patties. As you get to the last few burgers you'll find the heavier red pepper collects at the bottom. So it's worth bearing this in mind as you make the patties and ensure there's an even mix of red pepper.

2. Chillies do not always suit some children so instead add four teaspoons of mild sweet chilli sauce to add a 'hint of heat and a dose of sweet'.

3. When the burgers are first placed on a hot barbecue, leave them for a few minutes to seal. If they are moved too quickly – known as 'barbecue pokey syndrome' – they could stick and break apart. Eggs are often used to bind home-made burgers together, but I've always found that especially messy. So there's not an egg in sight here.

4. Cook for five to eight minutes on either side, until cooked through, then serve in a soft bun.

308

Burger variations

Why not play around with other flavour combinations with your home-made burgers? Pork and grated apple go well together, as does turkey and grated apple (you can also lay a thin slice of apple on top of the burger for added crunch). Beef and mustard are a classic combination. Or give pork and sweet chilli sauce a try.

309

A family feast

A bag of wooden skewers, believe it or not, is an essential piece of kit for any family camping trip and it follows the same principle as the tortilla wraps. If the kids won't eat it from a plate, push it on to a stick and it seems to change the whole dynamic. Kids (and mums and dads) can get creative when it comes to building their meals on a stick too.

310

Use a skewer

Skewers are essential for making s'mores (see page 194). It's a good idea to soak wooden skewers in water for 30 minutes before use to prevent them from burning.

311

Twigged it!

If there's a rosemary bush on your campsite you can even use woody rosemary twigs instead of wooden skewers to add extra flavour to food. They need to be of a reasonable size and strength, cleaned and stripped of any offshoots.

312

Halloumi and courgette on a stick

For a vegetarian kebab, drizzle some chunks of halloumi (the squeaky cheese), courgette and baby tomatoes with a little sweet chilli sauce. Thread them on a stick and grill until they begin to colour.

313

Sausage on a stick, camping style

For each person allow two sausages, six cherry tomatoes and a quarter of a red pepper.

Cook the sausages on the barbecue until they are just done. Using a sharp knife (and a fork so that you don't burn yourself), cut each sausage into four pieces. Thread them alternately onto a skewer with baby tomatoes and bits of pepper that have been drizzled with a little oil.

Cook them on the grill for another five minutes, turning, so that the vegetables start to soften.

Serve with this basic barbecue dip:
In a bowl combine 6 tbsp tomato ketchup, 1 tbsp Worcestershire Sauce, 2 tsp soy sauce, 2 heaped tsp brown sugar and 1 tsp smoked paprika.

Mix it all together well and see how it brings a tangy party atmosphere to all your skewered food!

314

Pork sticks with sweet and sour dip

You'll need:

300g pork steaks, cut into 3cm cubes
1 small tin of pineapple rings, cut into
3cm pieces and juice retained
1 red, 1 green and 1 yellow pepper, all
cut into three rough 3cm square pieces

Sweet and sour dip ingredients:
3 tbsp soy sauce
3 tbsp tomato ketchup
3 tbsp rice wine vinegar
3 tsp caster sugar
75ml pineapple juice from the tin
1½ tsp cornflour

1. Mix all the dip ingredients, apart from the cornflour, together in a bowl.

2. Spoon three tablespoons of the mixture into a freezer bag and add the pork pieces. Seal, toss together and put the bag of pork into a cool box to marinate for an hour.

3. Put the remaining dip mixture into a small pan along with the cornflour and mix together well. Heat it and keep stirring until the sauce thickens. Take it off the heat and decant it into a bowl to cool.

4. When you are ready to cook the pork, thread it on to skewers (pre-soaked in water for 30 minutes if wooden) alternately with the pineapple and pepper pieces. Leave enough room at one end for you to hold.

5. Cook on a medium-hot barbecue for about 12 minutes, turning them attentively and checking that the juices of the pork pieces run clear.

315

Lamb sticks with cucumber and mint dip

You'll need:

500g lamb steaks cut into 3cm cubes

MARINADE

2 cloves garlic, crushed and finely chopped
3 tbsp olive oil

Handful of fresh herbs, roughly chopped – rosemary, coriander or parsley
Juice of ½ a lemon

CUCUMBER AND MINT DIP

Half a cucumber, diced into very small pieces
1 tsp lemon juice

150ml full-fat plain yoghurt
5 mint leaves, finely chopped

1. Mix all the marinade ingredients together and put into a sealable freezer bag with the lamb pieces. Mix it around so the lamb is well coated and leave to marinate for about an hour in a cool box.

2. Thread the lamb onto the skewers – about four pieces each.

3. Cook over a medium-hot barbecue, turning often to cook evenly. Depending on how well done you like your lamb, this should take about eight to ten minutes.

4. For the cucumber and mint dip, simply mix all the ingredients together in a small bowl.

316

Apple and blackberry crumble, campervan-style

A large thick-bottomed frying pan and gas stove, campfire or barbecue plus foil squares (roughly A4 size) are needed for this recipe. For each person, you need 2 squares of thick foil, laid on top of each other.

You'll need:

1 large dessert apple or 2 small ones per person
A big handful of blackberries picked from a local hedgerow
4 tsp light brown sugar

A sprinkle of cinnamon
3 large farmhouse-style oat or ginger biscuits per person. If not, digestives are fine
Clotted cream to serve

1. Peel and roughly chop the apples and pile them in the middle of the foil pieces.

2. Squash the blackberries a little in a bag, then put them in with the apples. Add a teaspoon of light brown sugar and a sprinkle of cinnamon per person. Add a small splash of water to the fruit.

3. Fold over the foil to make flat parcels ensuring they are tightly sealed at the edges and look like an envelope, and pop them on your barbecue, in the campfire embers or in your thick-bottomed dry frying pan over a medium heat.

4. While that's cooking, make your crumble. Allow about three large biscuits per person. Put them in a freezer bag and crush with the bottom of a wine or beer bottle, or perhaps even a tent peg mallet (without getting carried away).

5. Check the apple has cooked (about four to five minutes). When it has softened a little (don't let it turn to purée), take it off the heat and turn the foil parcel into a foil bowl by turning up the sides. Be careful as it will be hot.

6. Sprinkle the biscuit 'crumble' over the top to cover the apple and add a dollop of clotted cream on the side. Tuck in!

317

Old-fashioned steamed pud

This pudding is great to make with children. You first need to buy an old stone jar from a charity shop, or better still, see if your grandma has one tucked away in the back of her cupboard.

This recipe serves 6–8

You'll need:

150g soft margarine
170g caster sugar
170g self-raising flour
3 eggs

Golden syrup or jam to taste
Currants (optional)
Custard to serve

1. Use a wooden spoon to beat together the margarine and sugar until soft and pale in colour.

2. Gradually add the flour and eggs, a little at a time.

3. Pour into a well-greased stone jar that has either jam or golden syrup in the base. If using currants, add to the mixture.

4. Tie a well-greased layer of double foil over the top of the jar.

5. Stand the jar in a saucepan half filled with boiling water. Put on the lid and simmer gently for about an hour. Check the water occasionally.

6. Serve with extra jam or golden syrup, and warm custard.

318

Chocolate banana splits

Cut slits in the banana skins and pop in some chocolate buttons. Wrap in tin foil and leave on the barbecue grill while eating your main course.

Spoon out after 20 minutes – and there are no bowls to wash up.

319

Bananas in custard

It's a simple but classic dessert combination. Sliced bananas mixed with custard, eaten hot or cold. It doesn't get much easier, or more delicious.

320

Go blackberrying

Take a walk with a plastic container to get the freshest of fruit for your campsite dessert. Blackberries also freeze well, so if you have a freezer compartment in your caravan or motorhome, take some home.

321

Pick-Your-Own farms

Look out for those rustic-looking hand-painted PYO signs by the sides of the road next time you're out and about on a camping holiday. Drop in and get gathering tonight's dessert with the family.

322

Poor man's trifle

- Slice a jam Swiss roll into a dish.
- Add PYO berries.
- Cover in cold custard.
- Add a nice big dollop of cream or crème fraîche.
- Crumble some flaky chocolate over the top.

323

A great start to the day

Here's how to make a glass of milk more appealing.

Take an individual 120g pot of yoghurt (full fat is best as it's nice and thick) in your preferred flavour. Spoon it into a glass, then refill the yoghurt pot with milk and pour that into the glass – it's a simple way to get equal measures. Give it a good stir with a spoon and drink up.

Try strawberry flavour or Greek yoghurt with honey.

If your child wants it sweeter, add a little jam and again mix well.

To top it off, add some finely sliced berries that will look good and taste even better.

324

Refreshing summer berries drink

Simply put a handful of your chosen fruit into a strong glass or sturdy plastic beaker. Pour slightly cooled boiling water over the top just to cover the fruit, being careful that it doesn't break the glass. Allow the water to cool down, which will let the fruit steep in the hot water and release all of its flavours.

Then top up with cold water plus ice cubes if you have them. Sparkling water can add a glamorous touch of fizz to your cocktail.

Summer fruits that make good campsite cocktails are strawberries, raspberries and blackberries – or a mixture of them all – but don't be tempted to add any sugar.

Other refreshing drink ingredients to enjoy are lemon and lime when left for 30 minutes in cold water. Alternatively, slices of cucumber and fresh mint again left in cold water for the same amount of time is also a tasty thirst-quencher.

These kids' cocktails not only look great, you can eat the fruit once the water's been drunk too.

325

Champion hot chocolate

Instead of settling for a vastly inferior powdered hot chocolate at the end of a bracing day spent out in the fresh air, why not challenge the kids to use some of their favourite ingredients to create the champion hot chocolate?

With this recipe, topped with cream and other sweet treats, the hot chocolate represents the dark of the night, the small marshmallows are fluffy clouds and the sprinkles are twinkling stars – it's campsite night-time in a mug.

For each serving you'll need:

4 squares dark chocolate (ideally 70 per cent cocoa solids). You can use regular milk chocolate instead but you'll need a little more of it and probably less sugar
Just under a cup of milk
2 tsp sugar
Squirty cream
Mini marshmallows

Sweet toppings:
The best mixed tub I've found is from a supermarket and contains chocolate stars, mini chocolate brownies, mini-meringues and gold curls. A dusting of cocoa also works. It's all the icing on the cake, sort of.

1. Melt the chocolate in a pan, stirring continuously to ensure it doesn't burn. In a separate saucepan, heat the milk, then pour it on top of the chocolate. Add the sugar. Continue to gently heat the mixture while stirring so the sugar melts and the chocolate blends with the milk. If using milk chocolate (try giant buttons), mix it well as there will be more oil that separates from the chocolate. Pour into your mug and decorate first with squirty cream and then those fancy toppings.

2. Use a spoon to scoop out dollops of the delicious top layer before sipping the hot chocolate. And then chill out as the day draws to a close.

3. Mum and Dad might like to spice up their hot chocolate with a tot of rum. Just don't mix up the mugs!

326

Frothy coffee anyone?

Coffee shops have been springing up everywhere in recent years. We've become quite accustomed to good-quality coffee in the form of lattes, Americanos and cappuccinos as part of our daily life.

That doesn't have to end just because of a camping holiday, though you will need to remember to bring the right coffee-making kit. So here's a latte for the grown-ups – it's how I've been making campsite frothy coffees for years.

You'll need:

- Moka Express-type coffee-maker
- Cafetiere (for the milk, not coffee)
- Saucepan
- Milk
- Ground coffee
- Sugar to taste

1. Brew the espresso in the coffee-maker in the usual way.

2. Once the coffee-maker begins to gurgle, remove from the stove. Meanwhile, heat the milk in a pan for the required number of mugs. Once hot, transfer the milk to the cafetiere and use the filter to gently pump the milk until froth appears on the top.

3. Pour the espresso coffee into the mug (saving a dribble), and top with hot milk using a spoon to prevent the froth from falling into the mug. I like one part espresso to three parts milk. Then spoon a layer of froth onto the top of the mug and add a splash more espresso for effect (try drawing a tipi design in the top). Don't forget to use a biscuit to scoop out any remaining milk and coffee froth.

To make a similar drink but cut down on the kit, you could make the coffee in the cafetiere while heating up the milk in a pan. Pour the coffee into cups, then tip the milk into the cafetiere to froth it up.

327

The last straws

Every kids' camping kit needs its own pack of straws as they have so many fun uses. And if nothing else, a plain cold drink can be transformed by the appearance of a humble straw – essential if your child isn't the best at having a drink. To make drinking fun, link them together to create a jumbo straw and see if you can successfully take a long-range drink.

328

Crafty straws

Drinking straws are great to use for art. They are easy to cut down to make arms and legs for characters, or they can be incorporated into collages alongside more natural items such as leaves and twigs. Glue straws together to make walls and roofs for model buildings, and get creative by adding recycled materials such as milk cartons and egg boxes. Cut different coloured straws into small pieces and thread string through them to make necklaces. The crafty straw list is endless.

329

Straw games

Who played the pea and straw game when younger?

You need two bowls or pots, a straw and some frozen or fresh peas. Then use the straw to suck a pea onto the end of the straw and keep sucking while you transfer it to the other bowl a little distance away. See how many peas you can each transfer in a minute – the person with the most frozen peas in their second bowl wins.

Alternatively, make a maze for a frozen pea with straws for the walls. Then use another straw to blow the pea along from one end of the maze to the other. You'll need plenty of puff.

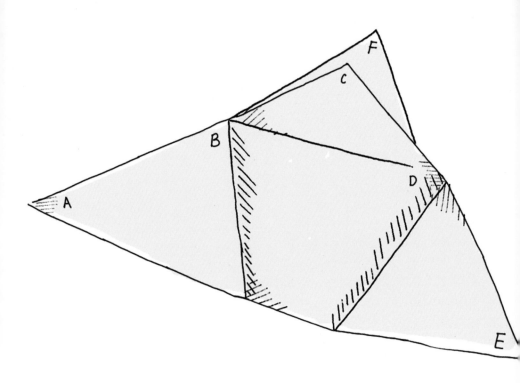

330
Make your own cup

Here's a neat way to make a cup from paper. The downside of paper cups is, of course, that they tend to leak fairly quickly, so maybe have fun seeing how long the cup holds your cold drink before the bottom drops out. You might be surprised!

First, you need to take a piece of square paper. If your paper is A4 size to start with, hold it with the longest sides vertical, fold the top left corner down to meet the righthand side, then crease. The bottom piece of paper that is left below the folded section is the part to dispose of. Open out the folded triangle shape and you have your square. Then fold it corner to corner to make a triangle (above).

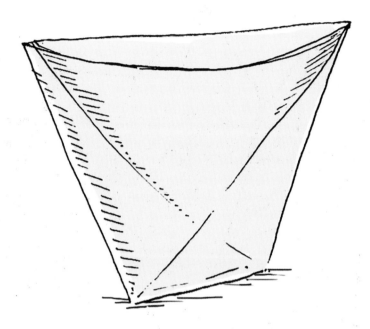

Fold point A to point D and crease. Fold E to B and crease again. Fold C directly down on itself and repeat that for F on the reverse side. Then open the top of your cup, pour in your cold drink and take a sip.

Try decorating the outside of the paper before you fold your cup, or use brightly coloured craft paper. Lining the cup with some tin foil will help it stay watertight for longer.

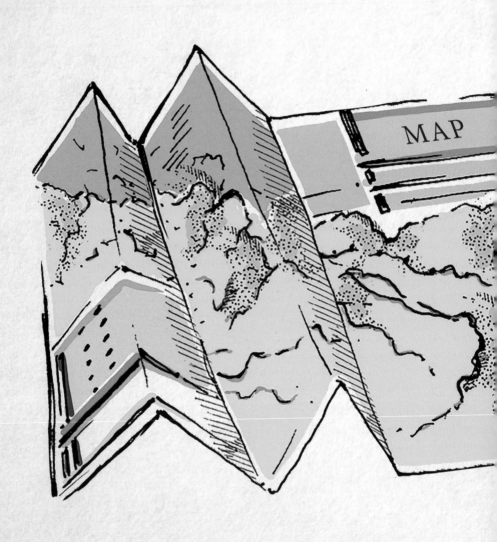

7
ACTIVE YOUNG EXPLORERS

"...here, in the call of the open air – with camping and hiking and the close companionship of Nature, comes the chance to test our skill and resourcefulness..."

Campcraft for Girl Guides, 1953

There's a very simple reason for the countryside and coast being an exciting and essential part of the phrase 'the great outdoors'. The clue is in the word 'great'. The countryside and coast are fantastic places to explore – a whopping great wildlife park, science laboratory, gymnasium and activity centre all rolled into one.

Children are becoming increasingly disconnected from nature and yet it's all there waiting to be discovered and enjoyed – and it's on the campsite doorstep. So let's start a mass movement that inspires our kids to become Active Young Explorers. We just have to pitch up and go...

Learn to navigate

The Scouts and Guides are great organisations to learn skills such as navigation. But like any skill, it takes regular practice to maintain – and excel – at it. It's essential to be able to navigate when out in poor visibility, at night or across featureless terrain and it's too easy to rely on technology. Learning to use a map and compass at a young age is brilliant fun and can set you on the path to exploring the great outdoors. I love looking at maps and there's nothing quite like the sensation of using one to successfully navigate from one point to another, especially if the conditions or landscape are challenging.

The sensation of cycling

If you want to be active in the countryside but take to the trail at a faster pace, swap a pair of boots for a pair of wheels.

We all remember that special moment when our children cycle without stabilisers for the first time. Two wheels and a lot of wobbling. Mum or Dad are running alongside until they themselves run out of puff while the little ones (hopefully) keep going until remembering to use their brakes to stop. There are the inevitable falls, bumps, scrapes and tears. But once mastered, cycling opens up a whole new world to little legs.

Cycling is great fun, helps keep kids fit and they love it. It also gives children greater independence and a wider area to roam and explore – a roaming area that's sadly

been shrinking over generations. And let's not forget that once you have your own bike and helmet, it's free too.

It's way more environmentally friendly than touring in a car and you feel so much more connected to your surroundings. There's the wind in your face, the smell of the countryside and the sound of birdsong.

So ditch four wheels for two with a hobby that can also be neatly coupled with camping. The two pastimes have been partners for a long time. Today's Camping and Caravanning Club had its origins in the Association of Cycle Campers that was formed in 1901. The Club's founder, Thomas Hiram Holding, had earlier played a central role in the formation of the Bicycle Touring Club in 1878. He designed lightweight cycle-camping kit and wrote about his exploits on two wheels in 1898 in his book *Cycle and Camp in Connemara*. It would seem that tenting and biking were made for each other.

Bound for the beaches

While you're on two wheels, why not cycle from the campsite to the coast, park up the bikes and explore Britain's miles of wonderful beaches? They offer a rich source of marine life to discover and some enchanting keepsakes to find.

Beaches have plenty to keep young minds engaged while reconnecting them to the natural world around them. Beachcombing, fossil hunting and rockpooling are three ways to learn more about the environment and have fun at the same time. And the great thing is they can all be free – you don't need equipment. Even with rockpooling you can just use your eyes to seek out fascinating marine creatures.

The bucket and spade brigade

Away from the rockpools, the sand itself is a source of great fun and fascination for children, not to mention their parents. The grainy granules are easy to shape into structures and can even be turned into striking pieces of artwork. There's an endless supply of free fun to be had, so grab a bucket and spade (and a few other helpful utensils) and head down to the beach. And while you're there, try your hand at making the king of all sandcastles – you'll be the envy of the beach.

Pincer movement

Crabs are iconic creatures of the coastline. Maybe it's their sideways walk or those nippy pincers. Either way, there's something exciting and magical about observing any living thing in its underwater world and there are two great ways to see them up close – crabbing and pond dipping. Maybe part of the attraction is the tranquillity of the water and natural surroundings, the excited expectation of not knowing what, when or even if you'll pull something interesting from the water – or just that kids love getting wet!

The great thing about crabbing and pond dipping is they are activities for all weathers. There's also a very high chance that something will swim into your net or decide to have a snack on the crab bait. You can take care of your catches in

buckets, have a good look at them and identify the species, photograph or sketch them, and then set them on their merry way again.

Crabbing has especially been a McGrath family fave over the years and our preferred spot lies on the Dorset coast. We've braved the coldest winter and hottest summer days to dunk our lines in anticipation. We've experienced both the highs and lows when it comes to catching the little crustaceans, no doubt courtesy of the weather conditions and the tide.

Sounds fishy
So you've mastered the art of crabbing and caught plenty of minnows while pond dipping. So how about setting the kids a new challenge: Can they catch supper? Or lunch for that matter. Either way, a plateful of freshly caught fish beats eating tinned salmon.

Fishing is a popular pastime that complements camping holidays, since many sites have lakes or fishing ponds. It's also an enjoyable way for children to learn a new skill of the kind that's often taught by parents and grandparents.

Sitting there with a fishing line in the water waiting for a bite gives people time. Time to simply chill out and think, or not think if that's preferred. Time to clear minds, young and old alike, and to notice the detail all around courtesy of Mother Nature – the plants, the bugs and wildlife, the weather, and not forgetting what's going on in the water itself. There is also the time to spend with your angling mentor, whether that's a grandparent or experienced fishing buddy.

Try introducing them to fishing at a young age and children could quite literally get hooked on the hobby. It also worth noting that good anglers are in tune with the natural world around them, from environmental changes to the weather and the shifting seasons, and that's always a good thing. Now, is there time for just one more cast to catch a whopper...?

Water load of fun

Kids are drawn to water and there's so much fun to be had in it, on it and around it, whatever your age. Rowing, stand-up paddleboarding, windsurfing, coasteering, water-skiing, snorkelling and even just paddling are just a few of the activities to try. However, for me there are two water sports that are natural partners for camping – canoeing and sailing. No, wait a minute, make that three – surfing (not forgetting it's little brother bodyboarding). Mention surfing and I conjure up romantic visions of touring craggy coastlines in a classic VW campervan, pitching up on a campsite and running across the sand, board tucked under an arm, to take on the waves.
The great thing about doing water-based activities is it builds confidence and you don't need expensive kit to enjoy our seas and waterways. Just some imagination, common sense and a love of the great outdoors. Water you waiting for?

Farmyard fun

If you prefer farmyards to fish, and dry land to water, then open farms are a brilliant way to learn about a variety of land-based animals face to face. They are fab for a

hands-on interactive day out and a chance to get up close to fun farmyard residents. A farm visit is an ideal activity for a rainy day as many convert barns into indoor play areas while the animals themselves are often kept indoors. Youngsters can feed and cuddle the little creatures – just watch out for those mischievous four-legged kids that enjoy having a nibble on a T-shirt or two.

Camping for all seasons

Having reached the last chapter of this book, you have at your fingertips a range of inspirational ideas for many camping and outdoor adventures. And that means it's time to try them out. With the right kit, camping can be a year-round pastime so set yourselves an outdoor adventure challenge spanning the four seasons. Each season will make you see the surrounding countryside in a very different light. Try something new, step out of your comfort zone and enjoy the smiles all round when goals have been achieved. Encourage friends and family to join you to share those experiences and introduce 'first-timers' to camping.

Try different types of camping accommodation, an alternative style of campsite or even pitch up somewhere overseas. And remember to get a good night's sleep at the end of the day. Make sure the kids to keep a diary or scrapbook of their camping holiday with lots of photographs and evocative captions. Show and tell at school will never be the same again.

Navigation and walking

331

Learn about map reading and compasses

To navigate accurately, you need to be able to read a map. There are grids of numbered faint blue lines on OS maps, which provide a grid reference.

Use the phrase 'along the corridor and up the stairs' to remember the order of grid references. The corridors are the eastings and this number comes first (the number reading horizontally). Next come the stairs, the northings, which is the vertical number. OS maps also have two letters at the beginning to identify the specific area of the UK.

Symbols are important to learn and maps have a key to explain them.

Maps are scaled down to accurately create a picture of the landscape. Scale is the relationship between what you read on the map versus the real distance on the ground. So on a map with a 1:25000 scale, one millimetre equals 25 metres on the ground.

Contour lines are used on maps to denote the shape and height of land. They identify features such as valleys, steep ridges, cliffs, spurs and shallow slopes. Contour lines link together points of equal height so the closer together they are, the steeper the terrain. To understand contours, form a fist with your hand and then draw some lines on your knuckles, linking points of equal height (effectively going around the knuckles). Then take a look at your hand from above.

To orientate a map, pick out a feature of the landscape close by. If a church is to your right, rotate the map until the church is also on your right.

A good compass goes hand-in-hand with a map and should come with features such as a ruler, scale measures, magnifying glass and orienting lines.

To orientate the map using a compass, place the compass on the OS map with the direction of travel arrow pointing along the intended route. Rotate the compass housing (the part containing the needle) so the orienting lines match up with the faint blue eastings lines on the map. This will align map and compass. The map can be placed to one side but continue to hold the compass still. Rotate your body until the compass needle matches the direction of the orienting arrow in the compass housing. You can then follow your compass bearing. Pick an object in the direction of the travel arrow at the top of the compass and aim for that. At this point a small adjustment needs to be made for magnetic variation, which in the UK can be between two and six degrees. Check your map for the current variation. Failing to account for magnetic variation can mean being off target even across short distances.

Step this way: The direction is sorted, so now comes distance. The compass ruler will help measure distances on a scaled map.

Pacing is another method with which to gauge distance and is especially useful when navigating in poor visibility or over featureless terrain. Before heading out into the hills it's good to know how many paces you take over a 100-metre distance. Here, paces are 'double'. In other words one double pace is from left foot to right foot and back to left again. The average number of paces in 100 metres is about 65, but this will depend on height and stride length. Work out your own paces and memorise it. When out walking you can then count the number of paces and when you reach your known quantity, you will have travelled about 100 metres. If you know how long it typically takes to walk the same distance, that will act as a guide too.

Some pointers: British mountains have markers, or waypoints, to assist walkers. Triangulation pillars, often called trig points, mark high points including many mountain summits and enable people to find their exact location on a map.

Cairns are piles of rocks on hills and mountains that act as markers, pointing the way to or from a summit. When navigation is difficult, cairns on some routes will be spaced at a specified distance, for example 50 metres, and allow a compass bearing to be taken. Walkers then follow the bearing, counting their paces as they head from one cairn to another, avoiding dangerously steep areas until they reach a path.

Things to remember

LEAVE THE STONES
Don't be tempted to add stones to cairns as new ones can be misleading. Stones also belong on paths where they help prevent erosion caused by walkers' boots.

TAKE A MAP
GPS devices are great and allow users to pre-plot and record routes, but as with any electronic device they can break or run out of battery power. So it's best to also take a map and compass together with the skills to use them.

PLAN AHEAD
Plan the route and tell someone when you're expected back. Ensure you get a weather forecast, and heed it, as the conditions in hills and mountains can deteriorate quickly.

LOOK UP
And remember, good navigation is more than just looking at the map. Don't forget to look up and read the landscape and scenery around you – and enjoy exploring the countryside.

Handy hints...

Tips for young navigators

A LITTLE POINTER

Fingers can be surprisingly big and clumsy when used to point out the detail or route on a map. That's where the humble blade of grass comes in. Pick a long sturdy blade and use it as a pointer to accurately pinpoint the spot on the map you're talking about.

LOOK FOR A LANDMARK

Binoculars are a great way to make identifying landmarks more fun. Ask your children to point out landmarks on a map, such as a church or hill, and then use the binoculars to take a good look. Ask them to describe what else they can see in the vicinity, and then see if they can pinpoint those landmarks back on the map.

CREATE A CLINOMETER

Make a right angle with your hand using forefinger and thumb, in other words form an L shape or reverse, depending on the aspect of the slope. Hold your hand towards the slope of the hill to determine a rough angle. You might decide that the angle makes the slope too steep to walk up or that you need to zigzag up using a traversing technique.

332
Use your watch as a compass

You can use an analogue watch to establish north, south, east and west, which are known as the cardinal directions, although you'll need to be able to see the sun in order to do this.

Point the hour hand at the sun, keeping the watch flat. Look where 12 o'clock is on the watch face and imagine there is a bisecting line between the 12 and the hour hand. That line points towards south, which means north will be pointing in the opposite direction. For example, if the hour hand is pointing at 4 and that is aimed at the sun, then a line from the centre to the 2 is the direction of south. The number 8 therefore points towards north.

333
Make your own compass

This is a clever way to learn the direction for north, and therefore determine the other points of a compass. You'll need a cork from a wine bottle, a needle, sticky putty, a bowl of water and a magnet. Cut off the end of the cork, about 1cm thick. Use the north end of the magnet to stroke the needle from the eye end to the pointed end at least 50 times, remembering to lift the magnet off each time. Place the needle on a small piece of putty and attach to the cork (or push it through the cork), then float it in the water. The needle will rotate until the eye end settles at north. If you're outside, you could place the magnetised needle on a leaf in a puddle, sheltering it from any breezes.

334

Make your own map

Tell the children to first imagine they are a bird looking down on an area. They then start drawing the map from the top left corner.

Identify north and mark its direction on the map. Draw features, consider scale and remember to use colour. Add symbols and write a key so they're not forgotten.

Start by making a map of the campsite. Then tackle a harder area such as a wood where it's hard to see very far. Encourage youngsters to describe specific trees and branches (having identified them first), then mark them on the map. Woods and forests can be disorientating places so a useful tip when exploring them is to regularly turn around and look back to memorise the way you came, paying attention to key features such as ponds, gates and fallen trees.

A highlighter pen can be used to mark the intended route on the map or to show where the family has been.

Climb a hill

335
Celebrate your local hill

Small hills can have surprisingly good views and still require a lot of puff to climb. Most areas of the country have a hill that regularly attracts local groups of friends and families. Their reward is a picnic at the top, a strong wind to blow away the cobwebs and panoramic views.

As a child growing up in Hertfordshire my local hill was Ivinghoe Beacon in the Chiltern Hills. It's a modest 233 metres above sea level but as a youngster it felt like the top of the world.

There will be hundreds of Ivinghoe Beacons around the country. Find yours and celebrate it with a climb to the top.

336
Good for starters

Take a step up from your local hill and look for nearby small peaks to get you going. I've introduced my family to Cat Bells in the Lake District, Kinder Scout in the Peak District, and the Malvern Hills. All are fab for a dose of first-time altitude appreciation and offer a new perspective on the little world below.

Handy hints...
What's in a backpack?

It's important to have the right kit when out for a day in the hills and mountains. Here's what I take in my 40-litre backpack (though a 25-litre-sized pack is perhaps more realistic for most) accepting I'm quite comfortable with a load on my back:

- Map, compass and GPS device
- Woolly hat and gloves
- Mobile phone with waterproof bag
- Two litres of water
- Lunch and trail snacks
- Fleece, waterproof trousers and waterproof jacket with hood
- First-aid kit
- Spare laces
- Penknife
- Spork (spoon and fork combo)
- Headtorch and spare batteries
- Emergency shelter (even if just to eat lunch out of the rain)
- Trekking poles (good for descents)
- Sun cream (we live in hope)

....

" 'Would you like us to take Cecil for a nice long walk over the moors?' he said. 'We can climb hills and jump over streams and scramble through the heather. It would make such a nice day for him'."

Five Go Off to Camp, Enid Blyton, 1948

....

337

Take on a tougher challenge

If you have caught the mountain bug, learn to climb by signing up to a course run by qualified experts. Indoor climbing centres are a good starting point, while rock climbing outside is often referred to as 'trad'.

Scrambling is another outdoor pursuit and is used to describe the point when hill-walking gets steep, exposed and rocky. Instead the trekker has to get their hands on to rock as well as their feet, though ropes are not required on easier scrambles. Given there are not usually ropes involved it is riskier than rock climbing and requires good judgement and an awareness of danger.

338

Learn the Sherpa step

Walking on steep or rocky ground isn't easy but there are ways to improve efficiency and technique. Step forward the Sherpa Step, which is also known as the Alpine Plod. This is a method of taking shorter steps to help keep balance and avoid muscle strain through overstretching. Look for additional smaller rocks to step up on to reduce the height of the step itself. Then revert to more normal strides on flatter, level ground. Try to get a heel on a footing for additional stability, and rather than walk directly up a steep section, zigzag along and up it instead. Don't go charging off at the start of a trek, instead get into a rhythm. When traversing up or down a slope, keep knees bent to have a more stable stance with the weight on the hill side. Trekking poles can also help with stability.

Invest in a good pair of waterproof walking boots with ankle supports and deep rubber tread for grip. Break them in first to avoid blisters.

Things to remember

LAPSE RATE

The weather changes quickly in mountainous areas so it's important to obtain a reliable mountain-specific forecast before setting off. A rough guide (known as the lapse rate) will see the temperature drop by one degree for every 100 metres ascended, depending on humidity.

LOCAL INFO

Obtain localised information about estimated rainfall, wind speed, temperature and cloud base height. If walking up into clouds, it will become wetter. It can also be much windier on summits and other exposed areas.

TRY ANOTHER DAY

Regularly assess the weather and if it turns really bad, know when to turn around – you can always come back and bag the summit another day.

Cycling

339

Take to the trails

An ever-increasing number of traffic-free trails are currently enjoyed by walkers and cyclists. The trails are family-friendly and take people to and through a vast array of places. They run through nature reserves, past ponds and alongside rivers, across viaducts with stunning views below, into countless places of natural beauty – and have plenty of picnic benches for refreshment stops.

Rail trails that follow disused trackbeds are fantastic to quickly transport you into the heart of the countryside. They are accessible and often flat to cater for the old locomotives that used to run up and down them, and where it gets hilly you'll often find tunnels to cycle through. The Monsal Trail in the Peak District, for example, has four well-lit tunnels, each about 400 metres long, which kids will love cycling through. Don't forget to stop and see if you can get an echo going.

340

Wildlife on two wheels

Although there's more noise from a bike compared to walking it's still a quiet activity and that means you'll hear the local birdlife. You could quite easily spot wildlife on your travels too, and it's easy to stop on a trail without worrying about traffic to listen more carefully, try to spot the creature and above all enjoy the moment. There will be 'traffic' in places though. Cycle in the New Forest and you may need to dodge the wild ponies, cattle, deer and perhaps even domestic pigs, which are released to roam the forest to eat acorns thanks to the ancient practice of pannage. It's a traditional form of animals helping each other. The pigs enjoy the acorns, which are poisonous to ponies and cattle.

341

Cycle-camping

Long-distance routes offer a way to clock up the mileage – why not take the family on a cycle-camping expedition? You'll also be a fitter family at the end of it. With a cycle-camping expedition the holiday can start from the front door. Or the back gate for that matter. Lightweight equipment is essential (think about taking kit that can be used for several tasks rather than just one) and there are plenty of tents designed with cycle-camping in mind, including some that will even accommodate the bike. Split up the tent between riders to lighten individual loads.

Storage such as panniers, handlebar bags and frame bags are important – ultimately you want to be able to travel light and far.

Get the kids involved with all the preparations including servicing the bikes beforehand and pre-planning the route. Select campsites close to the cycle route to avoid lengthy diversions at the end of a tiring day and at the start of the next.

If you don't want to lug much kit around with you, why not stop off at a campsite offering pre-pitched glamping tents that include cooking equipment? The Camping and Caravanning Club has a network of Ready Camp tents around the country that are ideal for that purpose.

342
Bikepacking

Once bitten by the cycle-camping bug, it's time to step up a gear and go 'bikepacking'. It's a relatively new way of describing more adventurous mountain bike camping to reach remote locations and is also an ideal way to enjoy more basic camping under a tarp, in a bivvy or rocking off to sleep in a hammock tent.

343
Choose a coastal route

There will be sea views to spur you on, plus the sounds of gulls and waves.

344
Stop for an activity

Plan a circular cycle route with a destination at which you can do an activity in the middle. It could be an attraction to visit or just the perfect spot by a river for a family picnic.

345
Sign up to a course

The kids can take road safety lessons and then move on to learn more technical skills such as finding the best body position during climbs and descents when mountain biking, and selecting the best route through difficult terrain.

"I say it is grand to feel that on the two wheels you can travel 60 or 70 miles comfortably, almost without being tired, carrying your kit and food."

Thomas Hiram Holding,
Author of *The Campers' Handbook*, published in 1908, and founder of The Camping and Caravanning Club

346
Take part in a charity bike ride

There are plenty of them aimed at families and you'll not only be getting fit but helping others at the same time. Or sign up to a guided ride to really get to know an area.

347
Join a club

The family will be able to enjoy the company of like-minded folk and learn from their experiences. The Camping and Caravanning Club has two Special Interest Sections whose members enjoy cycling – the Mountain Activity Section and the Association of Lightweight Campers.

348
Enjoy diverse landscapes from the saddle

Go on a bike ride that takes you through different parts of the country so that you can appreciate the changing countryside and spot wildlife species that are local to the area.

"The Machine — Any good average roadster will do if its owner will insist on a civilized handle-bar, only a few inches less than the space of his shoulders."

Thomas Hiram Holding
Author of *The Campers' Handbook*, published in 1908, founder of The Camping and Caravanning Club, and early pioneer of cycle-camping

349

Sense the change in seasons

Cycling is a year-round activity so head to the same routes but at different times of year. Appreciate the changing seasons through both the countryside and the wildlife.

350

Let the train take the strain

Go further faster by combining a bike ride with a trip on the train and it will feel even more of an adventure for the kids. You'll need to check for any restrictions on the train and may have to book a bike reservation in advance.

351

Play a cycling game

Think classic Hide and Seek but over a much larger area.

352

Go Dutch

Holland is famed for being both flat and bike-friendly. It's also a nation that loves camping. Put the two together and check out the country's 32,000km of cycle paths.

353

Camp close to the start of a big cycle race

Head nice and early to the race route on your own two wheels to get a good vantage point, then enjoy watching both the race and the 'caravan' of sponsors' cars and support vehicles as they whiz past you.

354

Go mountain bike orienteering

The sport combines map reading with bike-handling skills and you'll need to be fit. See pages 53 and 226–227 for more details about orienteering.

355

Smile please

Remember to take a camera with you to photograph those memorable moments or perhaps clip an action-cam to the handlebars to capture any off-road activity.

356

Use a GPS device

Bikes can be hired with GPS navigational aids fitted to handlebars that are pre-loaded with routes to cater for different types of riders. Pick a family-friendly route and get peddling in a 21st-century kind of way.

357

Experience a special event

Several times a year, before dawn, mountain bikers climb aboard a funicular train that takes them above 3,000 metres on Piz Nair, a mountain in Switzerland. They tuck into a hearty breakfast watching the sunrise before hitting the downhill trail back to St Moritz. Pick your special time and place, and pay it a visit by bike.

Handy hints...
For happy cycling

BIKE KIT LIST

Remember to give the bike a good service before you set off. It's also essential to take along a repair kit; spare inner tube; pump; front and rear lights (plus spare batteries or recharger); bike lock and key; and hi-vis clothing. If you do experience any problems, passing cyclists are known for stopping to offer help.

BIKE TYPES

Think about the best style of bike for the trip. Touring bikes should cope with smoother trails, otherwise consider mountain bikes or hybrids (a cross between a mountain bike and a road bike). Factors to consider include the type of tyres versus the quality of the track, suspension and bike weight. Tandems, tag-alongs and tow-along trailers are fun ways for families to cycle, though they do require more effort and balance. For youngsters being towed in trailers, remember to wrap them up warm – you may be hot from the exercise but they won't be. Trailers are also good to take along for extra storage on a family cycle-camping trip or if you want to stock-up at the local shop.

FOUR WHEELS CAN HELP

Buy a bicycle carrier for your car in order to explore far-flung places on a bike. The car will get you halfway there faster than two wheels. It will also be useful just to take the kids' bikes to the campsite. And don't forget there are many bike-hire companies around the country for a great day (or half-day) out.

ALONG THE WAY

Plan lots of pit stops for the kids, for example to visit an attraction, do an activity or simply to refuel with ice cream or a picnic.

APPY DAYS

There are many cycling apps available for smartphones that use GPS tracking to log a range of information. Use one to show the children the route you've cycled together with the distance, top speed, time in the saddle and elevation.

Things to remember...

ROAD SAFETY
Cycling is a great way for children to learn about road safety. Traffic-free trails are ideal places to practise bike skills.

COURTESY AND CARE
Be courteous on bike trails, and use a bell to alert people you're coming their way, especially if approaching from behind.

AVOID MAJOR ROUTES
If you're not on a traffic-free trail remember that B roads will often be quieter than the major routes. Canal paths will be quieter still.

FIT FOR PURPOSE
Always wear a helmet that fits well and it's a good idea for everyone in the party to have a pair of gloves.

START SMALL
Don't be too ambitious with a full-on cycle-camping expedition. Start small with shorter outings and build up to full day trips – and longer.

LONG DISTANCE
Get into a rhythm when cycling long distances and become skilled at gear changing – it will make a big difference, especially when it comes to hills.

HAVE A PLAN B
Always take time to figure out an alternative route if the weather gets bad or if the kids simply run out of steam.

REAR GUARD
Ride behind the kids to keep an eye on them – you'll also be going at their pace, not yours.

BRING SNACKS
Remember to take lots of drinks, snacks and a packed lunch with you to boost energy levels.

GET THE BALANCE RIGHT
Bikes loaded with camping kit will be heavier so the going will be slower. Keep the bike balanced and have practice runs first.

LOOK FOR SIGNS
Forest trails may have overgrown bushes that conceal direction signs so keep a close eye out for them. And take a good map and compass, especially if sticking to woodland trails, to avoid getting lost. Allow plenty of time between planned destinations in case of delays such as steeper-than-expected hills.

On the beach

358

Build a sandcastle fit for a king

Start by building a large 'volcano' structure of sand to form a strong base so that the sandcastle won't fall down.

As with a volcano, create a crater at the top. Pour plenty of water into the crater and before it soaks in, tap at the sides of the volcano to disperse the water around the structure. Repeat if need be until the structure becomes solid.

Next, create some towers for the castle. Put sand into a bucket of water, scoop it out when wet and shape into towers (different heights and sizes will add variety). For a tall tower, build it up in layers. By gently tilting a tower to one side, the water drains out and the sand becomes firmer.

Then get carving, working from the top of the structure down. This is where details such as parapets, arrow slits, gates, moats and even a portcullis can be added. A mix of turrets and conical roofs on the tops of towers will make the sandcastle even more impressive.

A useful tool to help carving is a bendable, shatterproof ruler. Hold at either end and scrape downwards on the sides of the volcano to shape a flat castle wall. Then use the end of the ruler, or a utensil such as a spoon, to cut away squares to form a crenelated parapet, which gives a castle its distinctive battlement shape. Shells and pebbles can also be used for decoration. And don't forget a flag or toy plastic windmill in the top.

Make sure you photograph your champion castle before the returning tide reclaims it. You could even use a time-lapse video app on a smartphone to show how the castle was built.

359
Bring helpful kit

All manner of objects can help create interesting shapes, textures and detail in sand sculptures. In addition to spades and toy rakes, you could try forks and spoons (use both ends), seashells, old plastic combs, shatterproof bendy rulers and drinking straws.

Handy hints...
For sand sculpture

Sand needs lots of water to hold it together so collect buckets of seawater, ideally just after high tide – that way you won't need to carry it far.

BEWARE FALLING SAND
Carve from the top down, otherwise the falling sand will damage the detail you've created below.

STAND BACK
Regularly stand back to see how the sculpture is coming along (and to admire your handiwork).

USE A RAKE
Rake around your sculpture once complete to frame it and help it stand out from the rest of the sand.

BE PATIENT
It can be like building a house of cards – somewhere along the way a section may fall down. The family's on holiday so smile and start again.

360
3D creations

Here are some ideas for creations that can be made from sand and then sat in or on to extend the fun. Remember to use objects to hand as part of the design such as spades, buckets, pebbles, shells, driftwood and towels (spades make great gear levers in cars and joysticks in planes).

- Open-top sports car or beach buggy
- Speedboat
- Jet plane
- Old steam engine (or take along a toy train set and lay the tracks through a dramatic sand landscape)
- Crab
- Giant sea serpent
- Turtle
- Furniture you can sit in, such as armchairs and sofas
- Mermaid
- Shark complete with big sharp teeth

361
Sand art

Create a picture 'painted' in the sand. Pebbles, seaweed and shells make great materials to enhance the design. Think about how shadow can add contrast to the picture.

Draw a large picture by scraping away the surface of the sand to provide a contrasting shade and use higher ground to get a perspective of it. Try carving giant footprints into the sand and then see what they look like from a higher vantage point.

Words are fun to carve out and can be turned into raised blocks, just like hot metal letters used on old printing presses, to spell out a message.

Use a paper template to make a picture. For example, back at the campsite draw the outline of a fish on a large piece on paper and cut out the shape to create a template. Take the template to the beach, lay it on the sand and then rake an area of sand to contrast with the rest of the beach. Remove the template and admire your fish picture. Add a few pebbles close to the mouth to look like bubbles. But don't stop there. Create lots of fish together using the same template to make an underwater sea shoal.

Frame your sand picture with four pieces of driftwood around the edge. And don't forget to photograph it – it will be tricky to take home!

362
Make a marble run

Build a good-size cone of sand and start the marble run at the apex. Keep the edges of the cone smooth (use that shatterproof ruler again) and carve into the side a gulley that spirals down to the bottom. Add obstacles to make it more challenging, such as tunnels, bends and jumps.

363
Build a dam

Streams or trickles of water often run down beaches into the sea. Use the sand to divert parts of the stream to create a new tributary or build a little dam from sand to see if it can withstand the pressure from the water behind it.

Moats around castles are also fun to make – see whose moat holds a bucket of seawater for the longest.

364
Go beachcombing

Every walk on the beach becomes a mini treasure hunt if you scan the sand for interesting objects. Beachcombing can be a rewarding and absorbing way to while away a few hours. And only take away what you need – leave the rest for others to enjoy.

Handy hints...
What to look out for

DRIFTWOOD
With its lovely smooth texture, pieces of driftwood come in all kinds of interesting shapes, sizes and colours. Full of attractive contours and variations created by the sea, no two pieces are the same. It's an ideal material for arts and crafts (see page 148 to make a driftwood boat).

PRETTY PEBBLES AND SMOOTH STONES
Pebbles with holes worn through them make great necklaces.

WEATHERED PIECES OF ROPE OR STRING
They could help with your driftwood boat, and you'll clearing the beach of litter that's potentially dangerous for sea birds such as gannets, too.

EMPTY SHELLS
They're colourful, make great keepsakes and can be used for a variety of artwork. Limpets, cockles, whelks and mussels are commonly found on our shores. If you are lucky enough to find a really large seashell, remember to hold it up to your ear to hear the sea.

WEATHERED GLASS
Pieces of glass worn smooth by the sea look like semi-precious stones.

SEA BRICKS
Masonry that has been smoothed and battered by the elements can make interesting artwork.

Things to remember...

A CAMERA
If you take your camera with you you can leave the find behind but photograph it first (keeping the camera well protected from sand and the elements). Large, heavy stones should be left on the beach for other people to marvel at.

WET WIPES
Great for both sandy hands and to help clean up an object there and then to get a better look at it before deciding if it needs to go back to base with you. Do remember that the beach will be owned by someone so you may need permission first.

Fossil-hunting

365

Find an ancient creature

Perhaps the ultimate beachcombing find is a fossil. The best way to go in search of a relic from millions of years ago is to join a guided group. That way budding young palaeontologists can learn how to carefully search for fossils and identify them. And kids just love a good dinosaur.

T-Rex and Co have a special place in children's minds. They get the imagination racing and can be both scary and fun – they're the closest thing we have to monsters. So finding a fossil and exposing it to daylight for the first time in millions of years is nothing short of amazing and a really exciting prospect for youngsters.

My family and I have camped in Dorset to enjoy a spot of fossil hunting on the Jurassic Coast, a World Heritage Site that spans 95 miles, not to mention 185 millions years of the earth's history.

We learned where to search (keeping away from cliffs) and how to use small geological hammers to open stones. Importantly, fossils can just be lying around on the ground. During our visit a woman spotted an amazing ammonite bigger than the size of her hand right by her feet.

WHAT TO DO

Learn more on a guided group and follow the Fossil Hunting Code – you'll find it online.

- Check first whether it's okay to search for and collect fossils in the area you plan to visit. If you find some, only take a few and leave the rest for others to observe.
- Use books, information cards or fossil apps to identify your find.
- Report significant finds to the local museum or heritage centre and let the experts take over. You'll be doing your bit to help the study of palaeontology.
- Jurassic Coast finds include a 16-metre long pliosaur, a swimming reptile with powerful jaws and razor-sharp teeth that apparently made T-Rex look like a kitten. Could you find the next one?

Handy hints...
How to find a fossil

Interesting fossils include insects, plants, fish, wood and mammals.

AMMONITES
Possibly one of the most recognisable fossils thanks to the snail-like shell. They lived between 65 and 400 million years ago and were free-swimming relatives of octopus and squid. Experts believe there to be 400 different types.

BELEMNITES
Squid-like creatures that first lived in oceans 300 million years ago.

GRYPHAEA
Today's oysters are distant relatives of gryphaea, which had two shells that clamped together. They are about 195 million years old and resemble old overgrown toenails, hence their other name – Devil's Toenails.

COPROLITES
Guaranteed to get a 'yuk' from youngsters. It's fossilised dung. Scientists examine it to find out what dinosaurs ate.

Rockpooling

366

Seek out marine life

They say the best things in life are free and that certainly applies to rockpooling. What could be more fun than carefully stepping over slippery rocks and stones with bucket and net in hand to find that jackpot rockpool?

The search is on for the prized pool that keeps everyone entranced for ages because of all the amazing creatures and plants that are thriving within it.

WHAT TO DO

- Do some homework first. Before you set off, learn about the local marine inhabitants and the best spots to find them, and make a list of your top 10. Identify them in the rockpool and start ticking them off the list. Before you know it your youngsters will be budding marine biologists.
- The biggest pools are often the best, with lots of rocks to look under. Lift them slowly to avoid disturbing sediment for a clearer view and remember to replace them carefully as they were found.
- Attach a small mirror to the end of a stick to get an undisturbed view beneath rocks.
- Make your own underwater viewer by cutting off the bottom of a plastic container such as an ice cream tub, stretch cling film over the bottom ensuring the film itself is taut and high up the tub (fasten with an elastic band) and dunk into the seawater for a clearer view.
- Go high-tech and use a waterproof action camera on a selfie stick that's synced to a smartphone for live footage of the creatures (see page 156 for more details).
- Don't forget to check out the seaweed – a crab might be lurking inside. The seaweed itself can be fun to identify if only because of the great names – oyster thief, peacock's tail, mermaid's tresses, rainbow weed and sea lettuce to name a few.
- When you've finished, be sure to return the little critters back to their original rockpools.

To learn more about the natural inhabitants of rockpools consider joining a guided tour, often known as 'rockpool rummages'.

Handy hints...
What to look for in a rockpool

There's a vast array of creatures to look out for around our coast including crabs, whelks, mussels, shellfish, snails, fish and the firm favourite with kids, the starfish.

STARFISH
There are 32 species in UK waters and yes, it's true, they can regrow their arms, and even their stomachs. They also breathe through their feet.

CRABS
Hermit crabs look for empty sea-snail shells to inhabit as their new home.

ANEMONES
A common species to spot is the red beadlet anemone. At low tide you might think it's a blob of jelly. When covered in water its stinging tentacles sway seductively in the water to capture its dinner.

FISH
The shanny, also known as a blenny, is a shallow-water fish that can live outside water for short periods of time as it is able to store water in its gill cavities. That means children (and grown-ups) can briefly hold them in a hand for closer inspection.

LIMPETS
These aquatic snails feed at high tide and return to the same spot, called the home scar, at low tide. And there they stick fast, so much so that engineers recently discovered their teeth were made from the strongest biological material to have been tested.

MERMAID'S PURSE
This is the egg of the dogfish, which is actually a member of the shark family. They are like square pockets and attach themselves mostly to seaweed or solid items to avoid being washed away. If you're really lucky you might see a tiny shark growing inside if you hold one up to the light.

Things to remember...

CHECK THE TIDES

Beachcombing, fossil hunting and rockpooling are best done when the tide is falling or low. Remember to be safe. Avoid getting caught out by the tides by checking local tide tables and learning about the fascinating subject of what makes the sea rise and fall.

367

Gone crabbin'

KIT LIST

Bucket, fishing line, children's fishing net, bait bag and bait.

HERE'S HOW

Fill up the bucket with seawater, a few pebbles and some seaweed.

Fill the bait bag with your chosen crab delicacy (the debate often rages within our family between the merits of raw bacon versus frozen fish). Securely attach the bait bag to the fishing line, together with weights.

Lower the fishing line and bait into the water from a pier or harbour wall (not too high up), or rockpool until you think it has hit the bottom (the line should go slack). Then wait. Give it a few minutes before carefully reeling the line back in, unless you first feel the line twitch. With a bit of luck you'll find a crab hanging onto the bait bag enjoying a snack. If you're really lucky, you'll have a cluster of them dangling from the bait (a group of crabs, incidentally, is called a cast).

Given there are no hooks, the crab is only hanging on to have a nibble at the bait. So either carefully pull him in on the line and deposit into the bucket or, if you have one to hand, use a fishing net to catch the little fella before he's had his fill and drops back into the water. Part of the fun and excitement is the sometimes tricky process of landing your catch before he waves a farewell claw at you and drops back into the sea.

TOP TIPS

- Frozen sand eels from a fishing bait shop is a top treat for crabs.
- Watch out for the pincers – they can give quite a nip. Hold the crab using a finger and thumb either side of the shell behind the pincers.
- Go crabbing in sheltered spots away from the wind, which can make them tricky to land.
- Add a stone or two and seaweed to the bucket to give the crab somewhere to hide, and avoid direct sunlight. Let some go before you put too many in the bucket – they don't like overcrowding. And change the water once an hour if you're hanging onto them for a little while.
- The little string bags that come with washing powder make great bait bags.
- When setting the crabs free, tip them out of the bucket close to

the water's edge and watch them scurry sideways towards home.

- When the crabs are biting, enjoy the atmosphere. There's always a bit of a buzz when lots of children are excitedly catching them by the bucketload.

- If you really get bitten by the activity, you could try entering a crabbing competition.

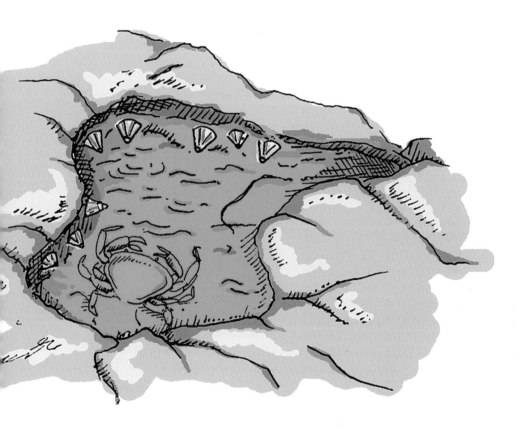

Pond dipping

368
Catch a tiddler

KIT LIST

You need a net, clear plastic container (purpose-made ones with magnifying lids are fun), magnifying glass, camera, wellies, creature identifying cards or book, notepad and pencil to write down or draw what's been caught, and a plastic spoon to pick up tiny pond life for closer inspection.

HERE'S HOW

Fill the container with pond water in readiness for the first catch. Pick a spot on stable ground and don't lean too far forward. Sweep the net gently through the water in a figure of eight shape to maximise the chances of catching minibeasts and bugs. Examine the contents of the net and carefully empty into the container for further examination. Ensure there aren't any creatures stuck in the corners of the net. At the end, immerse the container into the water and allow the creatures to swim off.

WHAT TO LOOK OUT FOR

Look for frogs and tadpoles, pond snails, dragonflies, freshwater shrimp, water beetles and pond skaters. As a child I spent many a happy hour catching stickleback fish in a stream close to home – it's one of Britain's best-known tiddlers.

Handy hints...
For pond dipping

TRY DIFFERENT AREAS

Try dipping the net into different parts of the pond such as near reeds, water lilies or in open areas, to see if the creatures differ.

SPOT BEFORE YOU DIP

Quietly look into the still water to spot minibeasts and minnows before dipping in the net.

KEEP IT STILL

Hold the net in the water and keep it still, allowing the water to settle and the pond life to come to you.

CLOSE INSPECTION

Use a plastic spoon to scoop up some water plus a tiny creature from the container for closer inspection, using a magnifying glass to reveal the minute detail.

OTHER LIFE

Remember to spot birds, animals and other insects that live above the water – they're also part of the life of the pond.

TAKE A SNAP

If the creature cannot be recognised, draw a picture or take a photograph to identify it back at the campsite.

369

Find some frogspawn

The growth of a frog from its start in life to springy amphibian fascinates children. The eggs are laid in spring so make a note on the family calendar to find some around March time, and then revisit regularly to watch them through the stages: hatchlings, tadpoles, tadpoles with legs, froglets (with a little tail stub) and lastly frogs.

Is it frogspawn or toadspawn? It's easy to tell the difference as frogspawn is laid in clusters while toads lay their eggs in long chains.

370

Action-packed pond dipping

Who needs a bucket and a net? Action cameras can add a new dimension to a classic kids' activity and allow youngsters to get up close and personal with marine life in its natural habitat.

Many action cams will work underwater (that's the crucial part so check first) and the latest generation models use WiFi to beam live images back to a smartphone.

Attach the action cam to a selfie stick. Depending on the set-up of the stick, the picture on the camera may need to be inverted within the settings. Hit record and slowly dunk it into the water (for best effect pick water that's clear and well lit by natural light).

Budding young nature detectives will be able to open up a whole new world of discovery by watching all those pond and rockpool dwellers happily going about their business without having to catch them in a net. And it's captured on video for all to enjoy back at base.

Start by probing just beneath the surface. A great artistic shot is to have the camera half above and half below the surface of the water. Gradually take it lower to see different creatures living at different levels.

If you can't sync up to the smartphone you won't know what you're filming, so keep the camera steady and let the pond life come to you. After a short while slowly move it into another spot and do the same again. It's an exciting surprise to review the footage a few minutes later to see what's been caught on camera. Did you spot a fish hiding beneath the riverbank or a crab lurking among the seaweed in a rockpool?

Try to identify as many creatures as possible and then edit the footage into a short wildlife film complete with voiceover to present to the family at a private 'screening'.

Fishing activities

371
How to get started

Look for an inexpensive starter kit that includes a small telescopic rod, a basic amount of tackle (hooks, floats, split shot) plus reel, fishing line and disgorger. Don't forget the bait too – maggots are sold in pint quantities.

To find out how kids get interested in fishing I asked a teenage family friend, Matt Brighty, who first started when he was 14. His advice was to begin with coarse fishing for carp, rudd, perch and roach. And they should be small fish – youngsters need to be regularly catching little fish to keep them interested. There tend to be longer gaps between bites when trying to catch larger fish because there's likely to be lower stocks in the lake – so keep the kids busy and if they enjoy it they'll stick with it.

Anglers should know what they're intending to catch so they can select the best bait and rig, and decide what tactics to take.

Young anglers find themselves learning a range of other new skills such as tying knots with great names such as the blood knot, the grinner knot and even the knotless knot.

What awaits the keen young fisherman or woman is a range of styles of fishing beyond coarse, such as fly fishing, predator fishing, beach casting and sea fishing.

372
Sea fishing

During a motorhome holiday in Ireland my dad and I took my sons Tom and Elliot sea fishing. It was an early start and our skipper wanted the boys to have a successful trip so we went in search of mackerel shoals. Each fishing line featured several hooks and within minutes the mackerel were biting in large numbers. The boys were amazed – and kept reeling them in.

The skipper kept the majority to sell though he filleted a number for us to take back to the campsite, no more than we could eat.

By lunchtime we were back at the motorhome cooking mackerel for lunch that we'd caught ourselves only that morning. It was delicious and created memories that would last a lifetime. My sons had learned an important life lesson – catching their own food.

373
Tune in to the environment

Anglers must learn about the environment the fish inhabits to successfully catch them, which means being in touch with nature.

How and where do the fish feed? What attracts them to the bait? Knowing the best fishing rig and bait for different conditions is a key part of the skill of catching them. For example, if the water is murky consider brightly coloured bait.

What will the weather and atmospheric pressure changes do to fish behaviour? The theory is that high and low pressure systems will affect fish in different ways, and the angler needs to know how to change tactics to match the conditions. Cold weather could send fish towards the deeper areas of the lake whereas they may be more likely to bask in the sunshine near the surface in the summer.

Rain can affect fish in different ways – in one lake it may see them head to the surface while at another they'll stay deeper. That's where local knowledge comes in.

Some anglers even climb trees to spot the fish when they think weather conditions are bringing them closer to the surface.

Fishing gives people the chance to appreciate their natural surroundings. Many anglers sitting patiently on the shore of a lake quietly awaiting a bite manage to blend in with the environment. It's the chance to identify birdsong, watch the bugs scurrying around your feet, and even hope a deer unwittingly comes trotting past.

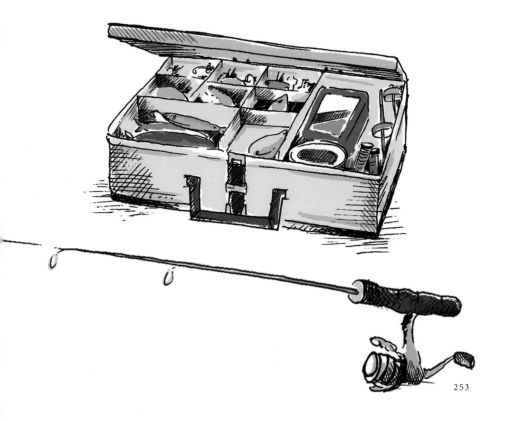

Handy hints...
On getting hooked

JOIN A CLUB
You'll learn from fellow members and make new friends.

GET INVOLVED
Take part in a work party. Fishing club members need to maintain their lakes and will spend time cutting back overhanging trees, reducing silt levels and restocking fish.

ENTER A COMPETITION
For many anglers fishing is a serious sport and there are prizes up for grabs. Alternatively, have a mini-competition among yourselves. Everyone puts £1 of pocket money into the kitty for the first fish out of the water or the biggest catch of the day.

374
Name that fish

Believe it or not, fish that are regularly caught in lakes can be identified and even end up with their own names. Fish with monikers such as Scarface and The Warrior tell a story and conjure up a battle between fisherman (or woman) and fish. So if you are lucky enough to catch a fish, don't forget to name it.

375
Rules and regs

Be aware of rod licence requirements plus any restrictions in place such as size limitations, season dates, bans, and what fish can be kept. Fishing lakes have their own rules, and charge for a day or season tickets.

Many campsites have fishing ponds or access to rivers that are popular with anglers. At certain sites, campers can even pitch up overlooking a lake stocked with a variety of fish such as perch, bream, carp, tench, roach and gudgeon.

. . . .

"The fragile cover between us and the sky, or the elements, is the charm, and we seek it for a variety of reasons, the chief of which is that having started it we soon begin to like it, and liking it, it is hard to leave off."

Thomas Hiram Holding,
Author of *The Campers' Handbook*, published in 1908, and founder of The Camping and Caravanning Club

. . . .

Water sports

376

Go canoeing

There's something relaxing about the sound of a paddle cutting through the water despite the effort involved.

My first experience of paddling was actually kayaking, which I did as a Scout and at school, but as I grew older my preference was for canoeing, a craft that's open to the elements. I just found it more comfortable and the craft more stable. Canoeing is a great activity that keeps you active, is fun to learn and can be enjoyed with friends and family.

It's also an ideal activity for campers. Many campsites are beside rivers, canals and lakes, making it easy to launch a canoe (there may be a launch fee to pay or a licence needed). My eldest son Tom and I have 'glamped' in a tipi before spending the day exploring the Norfolk Broads in a Canadian (open) canoe, taking the boat out on occasions at portages, which means carrying the craft around an obstacle. It was pure bliss for us both.

377

Learn the J-stroke

Canoes often allow you to have more than one paddler or passengers. With two in the canoe, you work in tandem to keep going in a straight line, one paddle being used on either side of the boat unless a turn is needed.

However, if there's a young paddler sitting up front, you might find the boat zigzagging due to the strength of the rear paddle strokes. That's where a J-stroke helps. In effect it allows the canoeist at the stern (rear) to compensate for the lack of paddle power on the opposite side of the boat, without having to switch sides with the paddle. The J stroke helps keep the canoe going straight without losing momentum. The stroke movement resembles the letter J and takes a little practice to master. It's ideal for parents to compensate for the lighter strokes of their children up front or for when tired little arms need a rest.

378

Go kayaking

Kayaks can be used for more sedate trips that canoeists enjoy, but their enclosed decks mean paddlers can also tackle faster-flowing, rougher and more exposed water with less risk of being swamped. With practice, that opens up a whole raft of faster-flowing activities such as kayaking on white water.

379
Learn a kayak roll

If kayaking is your thing you could learn the kayak roll, also called an Eskimo roll. It's an important method of righting a capsized boat but first you'll need to be able to perform a boat exit when the kayak is upside down. The best way to learn these important skills is on a course with a qualified instructor. A good kayak roll is very impressive to watch.

380
Camp and canoe

Combining canoeing with camping is great fun. You'll need to take a lightweight approach to your camping kit and there's plenty of canoe and kayak storage devices on the market that will help stow your equipment and keep it dry. Plan a family-friendly route over a period of days that offers a number of campsites on or close to the river or canal. Then get paddling.

381
On the wild side

Canoes and kayaks glide very quietly through the water and that means that the local wildlife is less likely to be spooked. So have a collective hush in the boat and sneak up on the birds

Handy hints...
Canoes or kayaks?

The two boats are different. Broadly speaking, a canoe is an open craft with the canoeists sitting on small seats or kneeling, and using single-ended blade paddles. A traditional kayak has a closed top, often with a spray deck over the cockpit as added protection from the water, and kayakers have double-ended paddles. Kayakers sit with their legs stretched out level in front of them.

in the reeds (not too close though) to observe them from a completely different perspective. Look out for rare birds such as kingfishers with their distinctive bright colours. Or will you be really lucky and spot a shy and rarely seen aquatic mammal such as an otter? I've even paddled around cows having their own paddle in the River Thames.

382
Make a day of it

My eldest son Tom and I once canoed along the entire shoreline of a large lake in a day. We estimated we'd paddled about 13km and stopped on a small island for lunch. Remembering how essential it is to keep an eye on the weather on longer trips, Tom and I suddenly found ourselves cutting short that lunch as the wind picked up, significantly causing difficult conditions around the island. We had a tough time paddling out of open water into a more sheltered area.

383
Set sail

Sailing is another pastime that neatly combines with camping and getting closer to nature. I once saw a snake swim across a lake as I sailed by in a dinghy. I gave it a wide berth as I made a few passes, amazed at how it was effectively skimming across the water.

Larger sailing dinghies are great for parents who want to spend time afloat with their kids, while there are plenty of smaller craft that can help children become independent when sailing single-handedly.

Sailing enables kids to learn how to rig a boat, stay safe on the water, set a course, race in competitions, tie knots, maintain their craft, understand the weather, and, essentially, harness the wind.

384
Become wind-aware

Your sailing dinghy isn't going far without wind so you'll need to learn all about it. Learn to read the signs of the wind around you – the sway of the treetops, the direction of a flag or the movement of the 'tell-tale' string attached to your boat. With practice you become 'wind-aware' and will more instinctively know from the feeling of the breeze on your face and the movement of the boat that the wind has changed direction or strength. If the water ahead is a darker colour with ripples or waves much closer together, it's a sign the wind is stronger in that area and you can both ready yourself and trim the sails accordingly. Being wind-aware is a great natural skill to develop.

385
Book your adventure

Recreate your very own *Swallows and Amazons*-style adventure by exploring an area aboard a sailing dinghy. Pack a picnic and maybe a small portable stove for use on land, and plot your passage across a lake to a distant shoreline or island (provided it allows landing) for tea. Many campsites sit directly on lake shores, making ideal locations to explore by boat.

386
Sail and camp

Many sailing clubs organise camping weekends so, for something a little different, try a sailing dinghy that doubles as a tent. *The Wayfarer*, for example, is a lovely boat to sail and with the right kit it can be turned into a tent.

387

Join a club

Sailing and canoeing clubs are great ways to share a pastime with like-minded enthusiasts while learning from them at the same time. Join an organised family day geared to getting kids safely on the water and building their confidence (not to mention Mum and Dad's) and having lots of fun at the same time.

The Camping and Caravanning Club has two Special Interest Sections dedicated to combining a night under canvas with canoeing or sailing – the Canoe-Camping Club and the Boating Group.

388

Bodyboarding

Bodyboarding is a great hobby in its own right or as an introduction to surfing. You use a light, short board and need to get your timing and technique right with the wave, not to mention balance, to surf along. Get it wrong and you'll be left behind as the wave ploughs on. Get it right and the wave can take you all the way back into shore where you'll be beached on the sand.

With practice and the right type of wave, you should be able to perfect moves such as the '360' (a 360-degree rotation) and even get some height with an 'aerial'.

I know people who have been bodyboarding for years but latterly decided to attend a surf school and learned more techniques in the space of two hours. With the addition of the safety knowledge acquired too, it's time well spent.

389

Surf's up

Take bodyboarding a step further and sign up for lessons at surf school. Starting off on the beach, you will be taught techniques designed to get you standing on the surfboard before heading into the sea. Surf school students will also learn ways to get the board over waves when swimming out, catching a wave and how to stand up and steer. It's also a good opportunity to learn from the professionals about beach safety, the power of waves, currents and tides, including powerful rip tides.

If you're lucky (unlike me), you'll be able to stand up and ride a wave on your first lesson. All that's left is to get checking the classified adverts for that classic VW campervan. Sounds cool to me.

390

Skim a stone

It's a timeless classic. Stone skimming is not about distance, it's about who

"We sleep with this end open generally, and as the head of the boat must always be put to the wind, either side of it can be used for ingress and egress. This is the door of our house afloat."

Thomas Hiram Holding,
Author of *The Campers' Handbook,* published in 1908, and founder of The Camping and Caravanning Club

can get their pebble to bounce the most times across the water. There are three main factors as far as I can tell (and I've skimmed enough stones in my time).

First, the quality of the stone, and by that I mean flat on both sides, not too big, not too small. Then there's the water. You want a millpond to maximise your bounce rate and if there are waves, you need to hit the gap between them with a well-timed skim. Finally, there's technique. Hold the stone at the edges between thumb and forefinger and crouch down to reduce the angle at which the stone hits the water (too high or too low and it can disappear without a sniff of a bounce). Try to get the stone to hit the water on its flat surface but at an angle so that it will bounce repeatedly until it runs out of steam. The same applies to you – don't over-power the throw until your arm aches and instead concentrate effort on technique and finding the perfect pebble.

391
Jump a wave

It's one of life's simple pleasures. Go paddling in the shallows and help little legs jump over little waves. Grandparents are great helping hands for added lift. Get it wrong, just as the wave is breaking, and you'll get a splash of seawater in your face. Get it right and you'll skip over the wave, but be ready for the next one, which is never far away.

Remember to respect the waves – they can be big and strong enough to knock everyone off their feet.

392
Stream fun

Little streams can be great fun. And not just for trying to catch a 'whopper' in a net. Collect sticks and build a little dam or use them with pebbles to divert a section. Look for natural materials to build little bridges. Use some string and practise knot-tying (see pages 98–100) to lash them together for a stronger structure.

393

Play Poohsticks

It's the classic game from A A Milne, the author of the *Winnie the Pooh* books. Each player (there can be more than two) selects a stick. They stand on a bridge over a stream and simultaneously drop the sticks into the water upstream (it mustn't be thrown). Players head to the other side of the bridge to see whose stick emerges first. The game doesn't need a bridge – just an agreed start point and finish line on a stream, and variations can include dropping in pine cones, for example.

394

Build a toy raft

Find about eight sticks of similar length and about the thickness of an adult's finger (put a ninth, thinner stick with offshoots aside for the mast). Cut two pieces of string, each about a metre long, plus a third piece about half the length. Use a piece of string to tie a secure knot at the top of the first stick, then the second metre length in the same way at the bottom. Lay the remainder of the sticks next to the first stick to make the platform of the raft.

Thread each piece of string under, then over the sticks at both ends consecutively, pulling them tight at each end and repeating the threading in the opposite direction. Do this several times to secure the sticks together. Once rigid, securely tie the working end of the string to the standing end of the first knot.

Take the mast and wedge it between the middle two sticks and secure with the shorter piece of string by lashing it to the abutting sticks. Pin a large leaf to the offshoots of the mast stick and set it adrift.

A long stick is useful as a raft prodder to unsnag it when it has set sail. Add additional props such as acorn crew members and a twig anchor tied to a fourth piece of string.

Make two toy rafts and play a game of Poohsticks to see whose craft crosses the line first (assuming they don't sink en route).

Things to remember...

LEARN THE WATER SAFETY CODE

It's important to be able to spot any obvious dangers. These include being aware of the water's temperature, depth (it's difficult to estimate) and pollution, hidden currents, difficulty getting out of the water caused by deep mud or steep and slimy banks, underwater obstacles or rubbish, and the absence of lifeguards. When by the sea, watch out for tides to avoid becoming stuck or cut off.

TAKE SAFETY ADVICE

Look out for any notices, signs or warning flags, know what they mean and follow the information.

GO TOGETHER

Mums and Dads should go along too and can point out any dangers. Stay safe and have fun together.

LEARN HOW TO HELP

If you do need to make a rescue attempt, first think about your own safety – you should never put your own life in danger. You may be able to help someone in trouble at least by notifying a lifeguard if one is nearby or calling the emergency services including the coastguard.

ATTEND A COURSE

Get started on a water sport by attending a course. You'll practise safety drills such as capsize procedures, and learn about subjects such as tides and currents, the wind, navigation including the rules of the 'road' and flooded river conditions. You'll learn the best techniques to make the most of the equipment and the activity too. Once you've mastered the basics, you can learn more from fellow water sport enthusiasts along the way.

SCRUB UP

Remember to wash off afterwards, including hands, or take a shower to get rid of potential nasties that can lurk in the water.

PLAN AHEAD

When enjoying activities such as canoeing or sailing, know the best way to get to your destination (and back again), stay within your knowledge and skill boundaries, wear buoyancy aids and use the right kit. Check the weather conditions and adjust plans accordingly. Always leave details of your trip with a responsible person, including when you expect to be back.

STOP THE SPREAD

Check, clean and dry-off boats and sailing equipment after use to help prevent the spread and environmental damage that can be caused by invasive non-native aquatic species.

On the farm

395
Sunday funday

Get a real-life behind-the-scenes look at agriculture on Open Farm Sunday, an initiative whereby farmers open their gates once a year to let people see how food is produced and the countryside is cared for.

396
Farmyard fun

Open farms are a brilliant way to meet and learn about a variety of animals face to face. They are fab for a hands-on interactive day out and a chance to get up close to fun farmyard residents. A farm visit is an ideal activity for a rainy day, as many convert barns into indoor play areas while the animals themselves are often kept indoors. Youngsters can feed and cuddle the little creatures – just watch out for those mischievous four-legged kids that enjoy a nibble on a T-shirt or two.

TOP TICK LIST:

15 must-do open farm activities

- Bottle-feed a lamb.
- Hold and stroke a rabbit and guinea pig.
- Feed the chickens and ducks.
- Cheer at a sheep race, complete with jumps and teddy bear jockeys.
- Groom a pony, then take it for a ride.
- Hold and stroke a piglet.
- Climb aboard a tractor and trailer for a ride, learning all about running the farm from the farmer along the way.
- Spot a young lamb gambolling in a field or pen.
- Watch a cow being milked.
- Let a goat eat from the palm of your hand.
- Get lost in a maize maze.
- Duck as a bird of prey swoops overhead during a display.
- Catch a creature with a net at a pond.
- Follow a nature trail.
- Learn to drive a tractor and digger (toy ones, of course).

Appreciate the seasons

Camping isn't just for the summer months and you will miss out on so many ways to reconnect with nature and appreciate the seasons if you confine it to warmer weather.

Instead, challenge the family to spend a weekend under canvas, or in a caravan or motorhome for that matter, in each of the four seasons in one year. You'll see the surrounding countryside in a very different light.

Each season's challenge should include new goals for kids and parents alike to reconnect with nature and remind themselves of the life-enhancing traditional skills and knowledge from bygone days.

Turn things on their head a little by visiting regions in a season you wouldn't normally consider. Give the challenge a name, draw up a plan that everyone gets involved with, and encourage the kids to keep a diary or scrapbook with lots of drawings, collages and photographs. They'll take all the prizes when it comes to 'show and tell' at school!

Things to remember...

COLD-WEATHER CAMPING

In cold weather, layer up to keep warm and to help regulate body temperature. Take a waterproof jacket with hood, gloves, a hat that covers ears, warm socks, waterproof footwear and overtrousers.

CHOOSE THE RIGHT TENT

Ensure the tent has a strong inner and flysheet plus the right tent pegs for cold ground. Tents with porches work well since you can leave wet clothing and boots in them to keep the inner section dry and free from mud. If you can, pitch on higher ground as the cold tends to find its way into hollows.

CARBON MONOXIDE DANGERS

Never cook inside tents or awnings. Fuel-burning appliances must only be used outside in well-ventilated areas. Never take a cooling barbecue into a tent or awning as it can give off lethal quantities of carbon monoxide.

SLEEP WARM AND WELL

Use a thermal or roll mat beneath a self-inflating mat and a four-season sleeping bag with a sleeping bag liner. Put a blanket under the sleeping bag for added insulation. Avoid wearing lots of clothes as it can affect the performance of the sleeping bag. Perhaps do 10 star jumps before turning in and some sleeping bag sit-ups to warm up first.

397

Spring

THEME

High hopes: Head for a campsite in the hills or mountains.

ACTIVITIES

It's going to be an early start (up with the sunrise) to climb a hill, so the night before make some trail mix snacks with the kids together with a breakfast picnic. Rise with the dawn chorus, quietly creep off the campsite and head up a known hill-walking route. Get some good elevation and keep your fingers crossed to see a cloud inversion while tucking into the first meal of the day washed down with a flask of tea.

This is an active spring break so perhaps also rent some Canadian canoes and go for a paddle. Learn the J-stroke along the way to help you keep going in a straight line. Chill out back at the campsite by enjoying a spot of woodcraft, making a tent peg in the process.

FOOD

There's the trail mix and also chilli and basil burgers that were made back at home – they're easy to chill and take away with you.

398

Summer

THEME

On your bikes: A cycle-camping tour following a circular route from home. It's a practice run as you want to see how you'd get on with a longer trip.

ACTIVITIES

Lightweight camping kit is the order of the day, so activities are based on little equipment required. On arrival at the campsite, get the kids into the local woods to build different styles of dens. Later, cycle to a permanent orienteering course to enjoy finding your way between control points using a specially drawn map.

Since you now have the navigation bug, devise and create a family cypher trail to add an air of mystery to the camping trip. Who's going to find the secret cache of sweets?

FOOD

It's summer and the barbecue is going into overdrive. So get skewering to rustle up a family feast on sticks. Think sausage on a stick or skewered halloumi accompanied by summer veg such as tomatoes and courgettes.

399

Autumn

THEME

A touch of glamour: Go glamping and get completely off-grid with a zero-electricity approach.

ACTIVITIES

You're up early again to start the day with a yoga sun salutation. The dawn chorus accompanies your stretching and mindfulness. Then make your own campsite weather station – it's autumn so there may be more rain to catch and measure. The leaves are coming off the trees so today's a good time to collect up natural materials for an afternoon of artwork.

You're on a glampsite so make the most of the fire pit in the evenings and gather round for a singalong and storytelling session. The nights are now drawing in, which means it gets dark earlier. Don the headtorches, wrap up warm and go for a little walk to see if you can hear, or even glimpse, any nocturnal wildlife – the damp autumnal ground may make it easier to spot footprints.

FOOD

The fire pit is ideal to bake spuds in tin foil. Then add some delicious fillings, followed by your own s'mores recipes for dessert.

400

Winter

THEME

Cool camping: You're normally at the coast in the summer so why not turn that on its head and go in the winter – it's a different, more exciting, time of year to see the sea.

ACTIVITIES

Play some games to keep family members warm and speed up the pitching-up process, then head to the beach. It's not the time of year to be sunbathing, so keep busy with some fossil-hunting and creating beach artwork. Spend evenings wrapped up warm outside staring up at the stars identifying constellations. And when it's nearly bedtime, make the family steaming mugs of champion hot chocolate and head inside to teach the kids some new card games.

FOOD

You've had a lie-in this morning, as did the sun. So why rush breakfast? Instead test out different ingredients in your own search for the best-ever bacon butty. And don't forget to take along the ingredients for the champion hot chocolate.

And yes, it's winter, so if a campsite doesn't appeal, pitch up in the garden. The family can always head back indoors if it gets too cold.

Index

Further Reading

A book of this nature has naturally drawn upon many sources for information or to verify facts. Given the wide range of topics, in places I have been unable to go into detail but listed here is a range of books, magazines, websites and organisations that will help further your own research.

GENERAL SOURCES

The Campers' Handbook, Thomas Hiram Holding; Simpkin, Marshall, Hamilton, Kent & Co, 1908

Campcraft for Girl Guides, The Girl Guides Association, 1953, www.girlguiding.org.uk

The Scout Handbook, The Scout Association, 1970, www.scouts.org.uk

Camping and Caravanning, the monthly magazine of The Camping and Caravanning Club, www.myccc.co.uk/magazine

Trail magazine, Bauer Consumer Media, www.livefortheoutdoors.com

www.youtube.com – great for practical demonstrations such as tying knots

www.bbc.co.uk

www.wikihow.com

GETTING THERE & PITCHING UP

Cool Camping: Glamping Getaways, Andrew Day, David Jones and James Warner Smith; Punk Publishing, 2016

The Happy Campers, Tess Carr and Kat Heyes; Bloomsbury Publishing, 2007

www.theaa.com/arewenearlythereyet

www.myccc.co.uk

www.thewildnetwork.com

www.ehow.com/info_12121901_fun-games-play-walkie-talkies.html

www.rspb.org.uk

www.getoutwiththekids.co.uk

RECONNECTING WITH NATURE

Britain Goes Camping, Don Philpott; National Trust, 2011

The Happy Campers, Tess Carr and Kat Heyes; Bloomsbury Publishing, 2007

Codes and Secret Writing, Herbert S Zim; Piccolo, 1971

Instant Weather Forecasting, Alan Watts; Adlard Coles Nautical, 2016

The Cloud Book: How to Understand the Skies, Richard Hamblyn; David & Charles, 2008 (reprinted 2015)

The Yoga Bible, Christina Brown; Godsfield Press, 2009

50 Best Yoga Positions: A Step-by-Step Guide to the Best Exercises for Mind, Body, and Soul, Parragon Books Ltd, 2011

OM Yoga and Lifestyle magazine, www.ommagazine.com

www.rspb.org.uk

International Dawn Chorus Day: http://idcd.info

www.woodlandtrust.org.uk

www.dbrc.org.uk

www.geocaching.com

www.ordnancesurvey.co.uk

www.britishorienteering.org.uk

www.metoffice.gov.uk

http://earthsky.org

www.girlguiding.org.uk

Royal Meteorological Society: www.rmets.org

www.gogoyogakids.com

www.nhs.uk/livewell/fitness/pages/yoga.aspx

RELEARNING ANCIENT SKILLS

Britain Goes Camping, Don Philpott; National Trust, 2011

The Field Guide to Knots, Bob Holtzman; Apple, 2015

The Scout Handbook, The Scout Association, 1970, www.scouts.org.uk
Living Wild: The Ultimate Guide to Scouting and Fieldcraft, Bear Grylls; Channel 4 Books, 2010, www.scouts.org.uk
Bushcraft 101: A Field Guide to the Art of Wilderness Survival, Dave Canterbury; Adams Media, 2014
The blog section on www.outwell.com
www.girlguiding.org.uk
www.writersdigest.com
www.nownovel.com
www.writerscookbook.com
www.sciencemag.org
www.forestry.gov.uk
The English Folk Dance and Song Society: www.efdss.org
www.folkgroup.org.uk

GAMES & ACTIVITIES
Hello Nature: Draw, Colour, Make, Grow, Nina Chakrabarti; Laurence King, 2016
Scouting Games, Sir Robert Baden-Powell, The Scout Library No 4, sixth edition
Camping magazine, www.outandaboutlive. co.uk/camping
www.nationaltrust.org.uk
www.english-heritage.org.uk
www.nts.org.uk
www.getoutwiththekids.co.uk
www.scrabble-assoc.com
www.todaysparent.com
www.forestry.gov.uk
www.wildlifetrusts.org
www.kodak.com
http://digital-photography-school.com
www.tots100.co.uk
www.proflowers.com

NIGHT-TIME FUN
At Night: A Journey Round Britain from Dusk to Dawn, Dixe Wills; AA Publishing, 2015
www.rspb.org.uk
www.bats.org.uk
www.goingwild.net
www.astronomyclubs.co.uk
www.getoutwiththekids.co.uk

http://liebacklookup.com
www.darkskydiscovery.org.uk
www.britannica.com
https://spotthestation.nasa.gov
www.nationaltrust.org.uk
http://earthsky.org
www.space.com

CLASSIC CAMPSITE COOKERY
Barbecues and Salad, Lorraine Turner; Marks & Spencer, 2002
Britain Goes Camping, Don Philpott; National Trust, 2011
S'mores: http://theplate.nationalgeographic. com
www.getoutwiththekids.co.uk
www.woodlands.co.uk
www.scouts.org.uk
www.netmums.com

ACTIVE YOUNG EXPLORERS
Bikepacking: Mountain Bike Camping Adventures on the Wild Trails of Britain, Laurence McJannet; Wild Things Publishing, 2016
https://farmsunday.org
www.britishorienteering.org.uk
www.sustrans.org.uk
www.cyclinguk.org
www.campingexpert.co.uk
www.getoutwiththekids.co.uk
www.rospa.com
British Canoeing: www.britishcanoeing.org. uk
The Royal Yachting Association: www.rya. org.uk
www.sandinyoureye.co.uk
United Kingdom Amateur Fossil Hunters: www.ukafh.com
National History Museum: www.nhm.ac.uk
www.countryfile.com
www.rspb.org.uk
www.anglerwise.com
www.thefishingnut.com
http://andy-kirkpatrick.com

Author's Acknowledgements

While reflecting on my experience of writing this book, a number of things occurred to me. One was that I am fortunate to have such a wonderful network of family, friends and colleagues. A book of this kind, brimming with ideas for outdoor family adventures, is thanks in no small part to their creativity, passion and knowledge. So I would like to pass on my gratitude and thanks to all who have helped with ideas and information, or encouraged me along the way.

First and foremost I would like to thank my wonderful and patient wife Paula, who 'lost' me for the best part of a summer as I indulged myself in my passion to write this book. She also reviewed every chapter and her suggestions for improvements have enhanced this guide. And to my two enthusiastic sons Tom and Elliot, who have got involved with *Camping with Kids* in so many ways. They appear in these pages in a number of photographs as testament to our many camping adventures as a family. I'm blessed to have Paula, Tom and Elliot at the centre of my life.

I have tapped into the knowledge of many. Ali Ray, author of the AA's *Pitch Up, Eat Local* and a *Camping & Caravanning* magazine columnist, has been unstoppable in her enthusiasm and passion for camping and cooking and a huge help. The great camping sage Clive Garrett, of Oase Outdoors, the company that owns the Outwell, Robens and Easy Camp brands (www.oase-outdoors.dk) never ceases to amaze me with his outdoor knowledge, which he has generously shared with me. TV presenter and bushcraft expert Andrew Price of Dryad Bushcraft (www.dryadbushcraft.co.uk) taught me much about this fascinating subject.

My mother-in-law Linda Neale and sister-in-law Lisa Swann, who have been involved in Girlguiding for decades, have contributed many ideas on a range of subject areas, as did Linda's sister Annette Minor. My parents Chris and John and sisters Nikki and Lucy have also been big supporters throughout my career – more than I probably appreciate.

Mountain Leader Dave Ascough (www.daveascough.co.uk) taught me much of what I know about safely enjoying hikes in our wonderful hills and mountains. I have stood on the summit of mountains with Dave more times than I can remember, and have always enjoyed his good company and sound advice.

Colleagues and friends Stuart Kidman and Steve Adams have been generous in sharing their knowledge, as have Mark Sutcliffe, 'Snapper' Ali Cusick (alisdaircusick.com) and Mike Finn-Kelcey. Thanks also go to Marie Sefton for her many words of wisdom and to old school friend Chris Moore for his advice.

Gav Grayston of Get Out With The Kids shares a similar passion of encouraging youngsters to enjoy the great outdoors and his website of the same name is a great resource for ideas. Jennie Taylor at British Orienteering (www.britishorienteering.org.uk), the folk at the English Folk Dance and Song Society (www.efdss.org), Claire Jamieson at www.sandinyoureye.co.uk and Kevin East of the Canoe-Camping Club have also been a great help.

We're never too old to learn and young people have much to teach us. For instance, 17-year-old family friend Matt Brighty's knowledge of fishing put my understanding of angling to shame. Thanks also to his dad Andy. Closer to home, our lovely village friends and neighbours the Watkinsons, the Chambers and the Forbes families have been a great help. Lynne's crafty creations are truly inspiring and all our families have had great fun testing out s'mores recipes together in the garden with youngsters Phoebe, Amelia and Rory. Meanwhile, Claire Hooper taught me much about yoga for youngsters.

At the Club, my Director Paul Jones has been a constant support from day one. Paul, the cider's on me. I've also received much encouragement from Robert Louden MBE, Sabina Voysey, Darren Whittington and Rob Ganley, plus my own Publications team colleagues.

At the AA, thanks go to Helen Brocklehurst for her ideas and direction, and to my editor Donna Wood – it cannot be easy to work with a fellow editor who is used to having the final say! James Tims, the AA's Art and Production Manager, has been a constant source of enthusiasm and creativity. Kat Rout has designed the lovely pages of this book and thanks to May van Millingen for her beautiful illustrations.

Special thanks go to Enid Blyton Entertainment, part of the Hachette Children's Group, for permission to use the extracts from *Five Go Off to Camp* by Enid Blyton, and the Scout Association and Girlguiding for permission to quote from their archives. The Scout Association (www.scouts.org.uk/get-involved) provides fun, adventure and skills for life to both girls and boys across the UK. Belonging to the Scouts offers more than just camping – from abseiling and archery to canoeing and coding (and a whole lot more besides). Meanwhile, Girlguiding also offers a wide range of enjoyable activities that develop skills and confidence, which girls take with them as they grow up. Find out more at www.girlguiding.org.uk.

Last but certainly not least, other friends who have supported me along the way are the longtime campers the Bakers, plus the Kumars and the Clarks (Rachel Clark taught me the delicious one-pan breakfast). Thanks to all for your advice, support and friendship.

The Camping and Caravanning Club

In 1901 a small group of camping enthusiasts held what was to become The Camping and Caravanning Club's inaugural meeting. Today it is the largest and oldest Club in the world for all forms of camping.

The Club has a network of nearly 110 campsites around the UK and also runs and manages a further 16 Camping in the Forest sites through a joint venture with the Forestry Commission.

Members receive a range of benefits including discounts on Club Sites; access to a further 1,600 member-only Certificated Sites; European and worldwide camping and touring holidays; insurance products tailor-made to all types of camping; the opportunity to join social camping events around the UK with District Associations; and access to camping meets with the Club's Special Interest Sections including the Photographic Group, Canoe-Camping Club, Mountain Activity Section and Folk Dance and Song Group.

Youngsters can sign up to the Camping Club Youth, which is also an official operator of the Duke of Edinburgh's Award scheme.

Each month members receive *Camping & Caravanning*, the world's longest-established and largest circulation monthly magazine for all types of camping. The magazine has its own website (www.myccc.co.uk/magazine) and is also available on tablet and smartphones.

Visit www.campingandcaravanningclub.co.uk for more information and to join.